THE END OF
THE NATION-
STATE

Jean-Marie Guéhenno

THE END OF THE NATION-STATE

Translated by Victoria Elliott

University of Minnesota Press / Minneapolis / London

The University of Minnesota Press gratefully acknowledges the funding
provided by the French Ministry of Culture for translation of this book.

Entire text, except Epilogue, originally published as *La fin de la démocratie,*
copyright Flammarion, 1993.

Published by the University of Minnesota Press
111 Third Avenue South, Suite 290
Minneapolis, MN 55401-2520

Printed in the United States of America on acid-free paper

Library of Congress Cataloging-in-Publication Data

Guéhenno, Jean-Marie, 1949–
[Fin de la démocratie. English]
The end of the nation-state / Jean-Marie Guéhenno ;
translated by Victoria Elliott.
p.   cm.
Translation of: La fin de la démocratie.
Includes index.
ISBN 0-8166-2660-X (hc)
1. World politics—1989–   2. Democracy.
3. National state.   I. Title.
D860.G8413   1995
909.82'9—dc20   95-13430

And there shall be a fourth kingdom, strong as iron; as iron shatters and
destroys all things, it shall break and shatter the whole earth.
As in your vision the feet and toes were part potter's clay and part iron,
it shall be a divided kingdom. Its core shall be partly of iron,
just as you saw iron mixed with the common clay; as the toes were part
iron and part clay, the kingdom shall be partly strong and partly brittle.
As, in your vision, the iron was mixed with common clay,
so shall men mix with each other by intermarriage, but such alliances
shall not be stable: iron does not mix with clay.

The dream of Nebuchadnezzar
Daniel 2:40–43

CONTENTS

PREFACE   ix

1
THE END OF THE NATION   1

2
THE END OF POLITICS   19

3
THE LEBANIZATION OF THE WORLD?   35

4
AN EMPIRE WITHOUT AN EMPEROR   47

5
INVISIBLE CHAINS   67

6
THE NEED FOR CONFORMITY   77

7

RELIGIONS WITHOUT GOD   91

8

THE GOLDEN CALF   101

9

IMPERIAL VIOLENCE   111

10

THE IMPERIAL AGE   121

EPILOGUE   131

INDEX   143

PREFACE

Will democracy survive past the year 2000? To ask the question while the Communist world is collapsing sounds like a provocation. But while no one is in any doubt that the fall of the Berlin wall marked the end of an era, we have yet, in order to measure the real extent of this event, to specify which era it is that has come to an end.

The "optimists" would have it begin in 1945. We had then, in the name of the struggle for democracy, defeated Hitler. But this victory was achieved with the aid of Stalin, and it was paid for with the servitude of half of Europe. Forty-five years later, the victory is at last complete, and the battle of ideas appears to be won. Who would still invoke Lenin to contest Montesquieu? Under this optimistic view, the development of political ideas has reached its ultimate phase, and the liberal republic, heir to the eighteenth century and to the philosophy of the Enlightenment, represents the most evolved form of human organization. Condorcet appears to have prevailed, and we are approaching the end of history, if it is in fact the case that history is above all a battle of ideas.

The "pessimists" contest this interpretation, which they consider simplistic. For them, the period that is coming to an end began not in 1945 but rather in 1917. The ideological parenthesis of the Bolshevik revolution is now closed, and we are witnessing not the end of history but the return of nations. Each new crisis that breaks out in Europe reminds such pessimists of the period between the two world wars, because for them, the chief threat is nationalism. Our triumphant modernity is threatened by the resurgence of history. We are haunted by the nineteenth century.

This book proposes a quite different thesis: That 1989 marks the close of an era that began not in 1945 or 1917, but that was institutionalized thanks to the French Revolution, in 1789. It brings an end to the age of the nation-states.

The cold war acted like a vast magnet on the iron filings of political institutions: For several decades, the polarization of East and West gave an order to human societies. In the Third World, dictatorships have survived thanks to their outside alliances, because they were at stake in the global confrontation. In the industrialized world, the question of our political identity was put in parenthesis—the order of the day was to confront the Communist threat. Today, the magnet has been cast aside, and the iron filings have become sparse little heaps of no consequence. This radically new situation does not bring us back to the beginning of the twentieth century, nor to the nineteenth. For in the meantime, powerful economic, social, and cultural forces have disrupted the circumstances that permitted the formation of the nation-states. In a world frozen by the polarization of the cold war, the effect of these forces on political institutions was checked. This effect will now be able to make itself fully felt. Radical questions will be asked, and the givens on which we have built our institutions since the eighteenth century will suffer a decisive jolt: the disjunction between our political order and the realities of today has become too great.

We believed in institutions, in the force of laws to organize and control power. We persuaded ourselves that the best way of regulating the social clock was to limit power with power, to multiply the poles of force, taking care to avoid all collusion between them. These institutional constructions accompanied the diffusion of wealth and power that characterizes the modern era. In previous periods, during the age of penury, possession was the only real source of power, and no distinction was made between economic and political power: to be powerful was above all to escape from the prevailing poverty. In comparison with this primitive form of "patrimonial" power, the "institutional" age seemed to represent inexorable progress. And now we will have to acknowledge the lack of fit of the existing institutions, and discover that there are, between the age into which we are now entering and the constructs of the Enlightenment, more differences between these and the patrimonial age that preceded them. We will have difficulty in admitting this. Because we have known nothing else, the words *democracy*, *politics*, *liberty* define our mental horizon, but we are no longer sure that we know them in a real sense, and our attachment to them has more to do with reflex than with reflection.

We are about to realize that, as the heirs of the Age of Enlightenment, we are inheritors with amnesia: laws have become prescriptions, the law a method, and the nation-states juridical spaces. Is this enough to ensure the future of the idea of democracy? We must ask today whether there can be a democracy without a nation. The great edifice of the institutional age has lost its foundation, and it floats, free of all moorings, cast adrift like a prefabricated building carried away by floodwaters.

The nostalgic citizens of the declining Roman republic appealed, not without grandeur, to the virtue of ancient times. Our lamentations today will not stop the march toward a new empire, any more than did theirs. In fact, 1989 marks the twilight of a long historical era, of which the nation-state, progressively emerging from the ruins of the Roman empire, was the culmination. This political form, far more European than is the idea of empire, has imposed itself on the world in the past two centuries, and we have taken for an inevitable ending point what is perhaps only the precarious result of a rare historical conjunction, closely linked to particular circumstances, and which could disappear with them. We call the coming age "imperial" because, first, it is succeeding the nation-state as the Roman empire succeeded the Roman republic: The society of men has become too vast to form a political entity. Its citizens constitute less and less of an entity capable of expressing a collective sovereignty; they are mere juridical subjects, holders of rights and subjected to obligations, in an abstract space whose territorial boundaries have become increasingly vague.

This age can be designated as imperial for a second reason, too: The idea of empire is not proper to Europe and is thus not the prisoner of our political tradition. It corresponds to a new age, one in which the European definition of politics will be seen relative to the success of the Asiatic world; it describes a world that is at once unified and without a center. The existence of a center recalls an organizing pyramid of power that no longer corresponds to our complicated world. We have entered into the age of complexity, without knowing if this complexity will represent an advance or a handicap.

This revolution of the laws of power first occurred in the world of business: the end of the cold war now permits it to expand into the political sphere; the whole industrialized world, from Washington to Tokyo, passing through Brussels, is discovering that the rules of power are changing. We believed that it was enough to replace nations with supernations, as a large enterprise absorbs a smaller one. We are beginning to realize that, as it changes in scale, power changes its nature. This book is a first attempt to explore a world that is still new.

Should we watch this world emerge with apprehension? It would be a great mistake to consider the age of the nation-states as an end in itself. The political organization that the Enlightenment bequeathed to us is only one episode in human history, the means that we found, at a certain stage in our development, to establish freedom in a political order. This definition of freedom will not survive the particular conditions that presided over the birth and the flourishing of the nation-states. We must, then, understand the rules of this new age, not in order to fight against it—that would be a wasted effort—but to save what can and must be the idea of freedom.

We are at the inception of the fourth empire:* both strong and fragile, closer to Rome and to the ancient world than to Christianity, it has been created on the ruins of ideology, and of that Soviet empire that once claimed to be the third Rome.

---

* [The reference is to Daniel 2, in which Daniel tells Nebuchadnezzar that his kingdom of gold will be succeeded by another kingdom, of silver, then by a third, of bronze, and a fourth, of iron mixed with clay.—Trans.]

THE END OF THE NATION

It may seem paradoxical to evoke the demise of the nation at the very moment at which the Soviet Union is breaking up under the pressure of nationalism, when the German nation is recreating itself, and when the United Nations has never before known so many members. More than ever, the idea of the nation is manifesting its revolutionary scope. Is this a return to the essential, or the ultimate throes of a political approach that has fulfilled its historical mission, and is less and less capable of carrying the hopes and responding to the questions of the day?

The nation is a modern idea, and the call for nationalism was the engine of the process of decolonization. The connection that, in the old Europe, had been established between national affirmation and the call for democracy became, when transposed to the arena of the whole planet, the link between national affirmation and the call for independence. The revolutionaries of the nineteenth century cried "Freedom"; the decolonized of the twentieth century called for "Independence" (in other words, liberation from the colonial yoke). So, for more than forty years, no one had called into question the equation of independence with liberty.

Yet for about twenty years, doubts have been surfacing. It began with the suggestion that independence would not always bring liberty, because it was not real independence: the former colonized nations were victims of "neocolonialism," which permitted the former colonial powers to continue to exploit them. Then another explanation emerged, which was first presented as a refinement of the first but which today is being found to raise fundamental questions about the very idea of independence. The decolonized nations threw off the colonial yoke only to fall into another servitude, that imposed upon them by the international organizations—the World Bank and the International Monetary Fund. Much has been written to try to prove that these organizations in fact protected the interests of the big capitalist nations, and in many countries of the Third World people now demonstrate against structural adjustment programs as they did earlier against multinational corporations and earlier still against colonial administrations. But is the demand the same?

In fact, through these successive changes can be seen a new claim—one that no longer focuses on the relationship of dependence vis-à-vis the exterior but on the capacity of national leaders to represent and defend the national interest. The call to nationalism of the countries of the Third World resembles more and more the national call of the Europeans of the nineteenth century: it becomes a call for democracy. In Latin America and in Africa, democracy and development are now linked; and in many capitals of Africa, people protest against leaders who have exhausted the moral credit that the struggle for independence conferred upon them. The fall of the dictators of Central Europe, and in particular that of Ceaușescu, is an example for the new African elites: the tribal model of the seizure of power by a family is clearly rejected. At the same time, the dialogue between Mandela and de Klerk opens for Africa the possibility of a social construction infinitely more complex than the rudimentary schemas that have hitherto served as the basis for nationalist claims. The nation is no longer camouflage for the tribe but a political space in which democracy can be constructed.

This great ambition gives new vigor to the nation, but does not succeed in saving the concept of it. The call for democracy makes evident the precariousness of national structures in regard to the objectives at hand. If the nation needs a state to become a democracy, where is the state in Africa? And sub-Saharan Africa is, on this level, only an extreme case of a situation that is becoming the rule in many of the Third World's countries in crisis. The legitimacy of the struggle for independence has disappeared and nothing has taken its place. All that survives in this landscape, devastated by economic crisis, are a plethora of governmental apparatuses, which function according to a patrimonial model of power that is increasingly being liberated from its national dimension.

The economy of drugs is a good illustration of this bypassing of states by transnational games that are far more powerful than are the states themselves. Everywhere that the state is weakened or the climatic conditions are favorable, drugs take root, profoundly transforming society. So it comes as no surprise that Latin America, but also Afghanistan and Lebanon, are important centers of production and processing. These days, the revenues generated by drugs are greater than the total public aid for development reported by the Committee for Development Aid—an estimated $100 billion. The effect of a suppression of the drug trade would therefore doubtless have more impact than would be that from a halt in the politics of public aid for development. Coca and the opium poppy are the only agricultural crops in the Third World that are flourishing. In some states there is no difference in the scale of revenues from drugs and that of the budget. With drug money, one could almost buy certain Third World countries; the public-interest sphere is now within the reach of private fortunes. It is, if one dare say it, an extreme form of privatization.

But what is a nation? Products of a European mold, we are used to considering the nation as a political form that is self-evident, a kind of natural culmination of all societies. It is time to realize that the idea of the nation that Europe gave to the world is perhaps only an ephemeral political form, a European exception, a precarious transition between the age of kings and the "neo-imperial" age.

A nation defines itself first by what it is not: it is not a social group, it is not a religious group, and it is not a racial group; in other words, what binds together the citizens of a nation is the product of a unique combination of historical factors, and can never be reduced to a single dimension, whether social, religious, or racial. What distinguishes a national community, as the Europeans have defined it, from all other communities lies in this: it brings people together not for what they are but for the memory of what they have been. A nation has no other definition but historical. It is the locus of a common history, of common misfortunes, and of common triumphs. It is the locus of a shared destiny. But a nation cannot be defined only by a single affiliation: if that were the case, it would be no more than an extended tribe. A nation, in the European definition of the word, is first of all a place, that is to say, a territory defined by precise frontiers, as precise as the boundaries that mark the limits of the fields in the old countryside of Europe.

Since Rome, the autonomy of law in relation to religion has established itself, thanks to the increasingly rigorous definition of the rules of property. To define a man by what he owns derives from law; to say what he is derives from religion. To settle the boundaries of estates, to establish a survey of lands, these actions are the point of departure for a law that is first of all a law of the soil rather than a right of individuals: this territorial rootedness of the nation has been the foundation of our liberty and the condition for an open community. This rootedness does not lock men into their communities; it does not become bogged down in the search for origins and affiliations. But its tolerance, even as regards the variety of men whose activity it regulates, holds it to the utmost rigor in the definition of the space in which it is applied. The liberty that it gives individuals—the actors in the social game—is based on the space that it governs. No ambiguity is tolerated. Through a play of communicating vessels, the genealogical, racial, or religious definition of a community must be all the more rigorous to the extent that its territorial definition is in question. And, confronted with this problem, we must admit that the solution that the nations of Europe have chosen is utterly unique, the unexpected result of a particular history that cannot be found anywhere else in the world.

The precise frontiers that define the field of expansion of the different European legal jurisdictions have a particular genealogy, which distinguishes the nations of Europe from all other human groupings that have misleadingly come to assume the name of nations. Frontiers outside Europe are, for the most part, far more recent, and were for long much less precise. Their sacralization is thus far more fragile. Decolonization was able, for several decades, to mask the unique character of the European case. The decolonized thought that they would be able to turn the idea of the nation against the colonizer, but the ensuing decades were to dissipate that illusion. Not that the Europeans were luckier than the others. Simply, because space was at a premium in Europe at an earlier stage, they paid for their "advance" by a millennium of wars, which permitted the territorial disputes of the old monarchies to be settled. A strong link was established between the notion of the law and that of territory: the law does not govern men, but men's activities, within a defined territory; if it were otherwise, men would not be citizens but slaves.

And even in Europe, the link remains precarious: Great Britain, whose insularity had from the outset afforded it a well-defined territory, does not set as much store by the notion of territory as the nations that have had to fight to establish their boundaries. England, similar in this to Japan, had for a long time an almost racial conception of its identity, which distinguished it from France and from Spain. As for Germany, a gateway toward the marches of Europe, its disputes with the rest of Europe found their origin in the definition of a German people that was not rooted in a territory, but in a language and a culture.

The straight lines with which the European colonizers thought they would be able to replace centuries of struggles have only really taken root in North America, and at considerable cost. There, it was necessary to renew the population totally in order to compensate with the force of the social contract for the artificial nature of the space that it governed. It was not enough (as the Organization of African Unity made the decision to do soon after decolonization) to determine the intangibility of the frontiers left by the colonizers to create nations within these abstract lines.

This is why, in a growing number of countries, the consolidation of the idea of the nation has become a priority of those in power. New founding myths are invented, as well as hereditary enemies, to try to reproduce at accelerated speed the history of the oldest European nations, forged with iron and fire. But these nationalisms seem highly fragile at a time that is no longer that of the building of great nations. We are far from the rivalries of the great imperialist nationalisms of the nineteenth century, which fought over the world for "their place in the sun," as the German formula had it. The national movements of the end of the twentieth century are engendered by defensive reflexes. They express a turning inward, a fear of the vast world that escapes us, and from which we cannot escape. It is thus hardly surprising that the nationalist spasm of the posttotalitarian world is xenophobic rather than imperialist. One could circle the world and show that, on entire continents, the national idea survives today only by allying itself with forces that have overtaken it: religion, race, ideology, and the tribe. Rarer and rarer are the countries whose genealogical history or social contract are such that their territory suffices to define the nation, like a given.

This is all the more so now that the "territorial given," in the few countries where history has been able to impose it, is called into question today by a combination of economic phenomena. The territorial foundation of political modernity, as we have thought of it for centuries, is under attack today from new forms of economic modernity.

"Territory" (spatial proximity) is of dwindling importance, now that not only agriculture but industry, too, represents a decreasing part of economic activity. To be master of the cultivable land in order to be able to feed oneself was for long the principal political objective of men who had become sedentary. As industry developed, the control of raw materials on the one hand and the necessity to gather thousands of men in the mines on the other contributed to link economic activity to a certain organization of space. Because industry dealt in cumbersome materials and concentrated large numbers of men in one place, space was of the essence. In an automobile—the characteristic industrial product of the first half of the twentieth century—raw materials represent 30 percent to 40 percent of its value. In an electronic component, the symbol of the new age, raw materials barely represent 1 percent.

This means that the world is becoming more "abstract," more "immaterial." Wealth has become less and less tangible. In the formation of value, it is more and more difficult to localize its material components. And value is based on the capacity to be accessed. Someone who has access to the files of the fifty thousand richest people in France is wealthier than the jeweler who owns a gold brooch: as soon as penury disappeared, value was created in bringing together the right offer with the right demand. So, with the revolution in telecommunications, the network is divested of territoriality: we have passed from a network of navigable waterways and railroads to an infrastructure of air transport and telecommunications that has profoundly upset the notion of space. In his economic activity, the IBM executive, wherever in the world he finds himself, may tap into the electronic network of his company and is as "plugged in" as the farmer in Périgord is to the village that he has never left. The essential is not to master a territory but to have access to a network. This transformation also explains why men have again become mobile. The process of sed-entarization of the past few centuries has ended, and migrations are under way again. Industry does not necessarily install itself where labor is abundant. Men go where wealth is created: Migra-tions of the poor, in a world in which one is no longer rooted to a plot of earth except by police constraint, are beginning to be-come a major fact in the economy, but also in political life as it is to redefine itself in the coming century.

This revolution of the economy diminishes the value of space and increases the value of men—for rarity, which determines value, has changed, for space as it has for men: the space that is now at a premium is that where actual meetings can take place (hence the gulf between the great capitals of the world and that of the cities left out of the loop) and leisure space. Natural beauty close to urban centers is priceless, as can be seen on the French Riviera. Value is less and less associated with production; the price of agricultural land is in steady decline. The logic of the immate-rial economy thus affects that which seems to have escaped it: the soil. From now on, a piece of land is worth less for what it can produce than for the people who can settle on it. The inhabitants have in effect become a resource that is at once most abundant and most rare: it has never been as easy to procure cheap, un-skilled labor. Never has competence been as sought after, since it has become the object of competition at a global level.

Such a reversal of perspectives will have profound conse-quences on the political order. The scarcity of space was the foun-dation of our law. It was this that gave rise to the land survey, and to the Italian cities, ancestors of the modern democracy. And the abundance of men has liberated us from slavery. These two phenomena are at the origin of the modern nation. What new political order will grow out of a situation that is so profoundly different?

We already have a glimpse of it in the fiscal sphere, which is all the more significant in that the authority to levy taxes and the control of this authority constituted the first elements of the institutionalization of power, and in that European national democracy was built on this struggle. In all the modern democracies, taxation has a territorial basis, whether it affects wealth, transactions, or persons. This logic is called into question today on three counts: First because people have become increasingly mobile—moving to avoid taxes if they are rich, to sell their competence at a higher price if they have a particular talent, and to find work if they are poor. Then, because capital is at once mobile and in short supply, the desire to attract foreign capital makes it difficult to control a nation's capital. Finally because, in the age of the multinational corporations, which tend to locate the different phases of production of a single product over several countries, the attribution of added value becomes more and more problematic, taking into account the uncertainty that hangs over the price of internal transfer. When there is no longer a territorial imperative, when the place of residence and the investment are no longer a given but a choice, when added value is generated in too abstract a fashion for its creation to be assigned to a precise location, taxation is no longer a sovereign decision. Certainly, there still exist vast domains of economic activity that are not liberated from territorial constraints, and the state guards all authority to tax real estate or workers attached to a factory. But as soon as it undertakes to tax new forms of the creation of wealth, the national state is in competition with the whole world, and it cannot with impunity demand more taxes than its competitors in the rush for capital and talent. And if the gap between the fiscal pressure imposed on those who cannot liberate themselves from territorial constraints and those who can escape them becomes too glaring, the political coherence of the fiscal system is likely to create difficulties. One cannot for long tax workers' income three times more than income from capital. So, even where it still believes itself to be sovereign, the nation-state has to give in to a new constraint, which distorts the relationship that had hitherto been established, through taxes, between the citizens and the nation.

Taxes, to retain a shred of legitimacy, must be presented as playing only a modest role: the simple counterweight of the benefits in "collective wealth" provided by the state, not as an expression of the measure of cohesion in the body politic. Without provoking the flight of capital and talent abroad, a state cannot allow itself to increase taxes above the level of that in comparable countries. Some will see in this constraint a happy application in the political domain of the laws of the market. In fact, because the benefit of numerous collective services (security, infrastructure, justice) is not linked to the payment of taxes, many enterprises will be able to limit their fiscal burden, while establishing themselves in states that offer the best collective benefits. The calling into question of the territorial basis of taxation thus has far more fundamental consequences than a superficial liberalism would suggest. It signifies the impoverishment of the nation-states and their incapacity to finance collective services by taxation. Either the states that offer comparable benefits agree not to engage in "fiscal competition," and accept the mechanisms of equalization, or states reduce their collective "free" services and replace them with paying benefits or individualized systems of insurance.

In each of these hypotheses, the nation is threatened as the natural space of solidarity and political control.

Poorly equipped to collect taxes, the nation is hardly more efficient in managing its expenses. In the case of the daily needs of its inhabitants, it is too remote, being at once unable efficiently to supervise the disbursement of public funds and protected from real political control. Who would think to overturn a government because the public school or hospital in their town no longer gives satisfaction? It is well known that the central administration cannot do anything, even if it is just as plain that it is the source of funds. No one trusts a national official to manage equitably the even distribution of resources, let alone administer public services directly. Concern for efficient management makes an entity that is administered, financed, and controlled at the local level more attractive; it is thus of little importance that, by giving preference to proximity, one is taking the risk that the rich become richer and the poor poorer. One identifies only with what one can control, and the modern nation-state, in its day-to-day management, seems uncontrollable, and hence irresponsible. The rich Lombards no longer want their tax monies to be wasted in Naples. Solidarity is all the more difficult to accept if one is no longer confident that the state will administer it efficiently. At all levels of political organization, the same resistance appears: The rich suburbs no longer wish to underwrite the poor suburbs. Any subsidy causes a problem; the common space of politics has lost its legitimacy, and in its crisis brings down with it the notion of national solidarity; and no one knows whether this loss of legitimacy is due to the failures of the nation-state or to more profound doubts about the national community that it claims to administer.

Too remote to manage the problems of our daily life, the nation nevertheless remains too constrained to confront the global problems that affect us. Whether it is a question of the traditional functions of sovereignty, like defense or justice, or of economic competences, the nation appears increasingly like a straitjacket, poorly adapted to the growing integration of the world.

As regards defense, two states, the Soviet Union and the United States, have claimed for forty years not to rely on anyone but themselves to ensure their defense. At the opposite pole, the two losers of World War II, making virtue of necessity, devoted only a limited part of their reserves to defense, and left to the United States the responsibility for organizing the world and guaranteeing their security. It is now clear who won and who lost. The Soviet Union exhausted itself in a race in which it was obliged to devote a growing portion of its national product to its military budget. The United States fared better, and was able for a long time to reconcile prosperity and defense. But in its turn, the United States suffered the consequences of its solitary effort, and no one doubts that it will require a significant reduction in its military budget and a massive reorientation of public expenditure if it is to avoid decline. The optimists say that the demise of the Soviet Union comes at exactly the right time to permit such a reduction without excessive risks. Nothing could be less certain: the equalizing power of technology—which renders the most sophisticated weapons as easy to use as an old nineteenth-century rifle, allowing a terrorist with a Stinger missile to shoot down an airliner, and which, with the proliferation of long-range missiles, exposes us to the reach of countries far from our frontiers—creates new threats. And these threats come just as the increase of exchanges and interdependency, with growing sophistication of the developed economies, renders us more vulnerable.

More than ever, in fact, prosperity demands order. In a world in which complexity has been divided into a multitude of simple operations, in which wealth grows out of the multiplication of connections, it is imperative to avoid disruption, the unforeseen, the uncertain, the uncontrollable. There must be an order—an order that is not just the natural fruit of economic interdependence but one that depends also on the force of armies. But how can the United States keep its place if it must spend on defense a share of its resources that is always greater than that of its direct competitors? The acrimonious exchanges between Tokyo and Washington that were provoked by the Gulf crisis show that America no longer has the means to be the benevolent guardian of world order, but is loath to be the mercenary of the nonmilitary powers. Russia, whose only real and immediately mobilizable asset is military power, will perhaps be disposed to play this role. But the community of nations is not ready to entrust to either one of these countries the responsibility for ensuring world peace.

In effect, no nation, however powerful, can single-handedly guarantee stability. No nation has both the confidence of the others and the means lastingly to fulfill this role without running the risk of weakening or yielding to the temptation to abuse the responsibility entrusted to it. Even if a nation has the means to ensure the order that we now feel the need for, it no longer has the legitimacy to do so. Public opinion in the advanced nations rejects all unilateral action; and the national interest, in the case of a hypothetical European nation, is no longer accepted as a sufficient basis for action outside its borders. Legitimacy demands the multilateral framework of the community of nations. The nation is no longer the natural framework of security, and we are beginning to dream again, so far unsuccessfully, of a world government.

The same observation can be made for justice: no juridical system can claim to be immune from international influences, as the increasing importance of the law elaborated in Brussels in the regulation of the different countries of the European Union clearly shows. This constraint is not only the consequence of an institutional construction resulting from a political will. It reflects the evolution of economies and the need to conform to international norms, which define themselves on a supranational level: a country that isolates itself within particular juridical norms, believing that it will protect its industry from incursions from abroad, deals its industries a fatal blow, for it seals its cutting-edge industries within a market too restricted to allow for the amortization of research expenditures and the development necessary to maintain competitivity.

It is in fact in the economic domain that the constraints of the national framework appear most strikingly. Each technological revolution has led to an increase in the cost of industrial research and development. One hundred years ago, the very idea of national funding for research would have appeared strange. The scholar in his laboratory was the engine of scientific progress. Research was within the capacity of the individual, and was a fortiori entirely compatible with that of an enterprise. The acceleration of scientific progress, stimulated in part by the two world wars, led to increased involvement by the states, which, through the influence of military budgets and subsidies for research, became the principal engines of scientific progress. The scale of expenditures changed, and, directly or indirectly, the great industrial concerns profited from public support. With the new programs of research in basic physics—essential to progress in electronics—and in biology, a new stage was reached: no nation, even one the size of the

United States, has the means to finance the requisite efforts on its own. Global cooperation has become a necessity, as can be seen with the Super-Concorde project or with certain research projects in basic physics (for example, giant particle accelerators).

The "territorial given" is outmoded, and no utilitarian, functional vision of the state can replace it. We can certainly congratulate ourselves that the modern states have lost their pride and are constrained, no less than any other enterprise, to try to prove their usefulness by running big publicity campaigns. This "reconversion" is not without its dangers. Is it a question of a simple recalibration? Between the providential state (which claims to do everything and does it badly) and the libertarians (who are convinced that the state can do nothing well) is there not room for a middle way—one that redistributes responsibility on different levels, according to the nature of the problems at hand? Such a compromise—surprising to the French, who are used to a centralized state—is at the heart of the federal experience of the United States or of postwar Germany.

Let us not be mistaken, however. The movement that we are witnessing goes farther than classical federalism. Federalism grew out of an age in which immediate dependence on the soil still dominated social relations. The different levels of solidarity that it aspired to organize obeyed a geographical logic: the commune inserted itself into the region, which inserted itself into the federal state. And this pyramid of responsibilities, determined by geography, permitted a political life to be organized, on several levels: there was a space for communal solidarity, a space for regional solidarity, a space for national solidarity; and, at each of these levels, citizens established priorities, made choices, and, above all, expressed a common will. This was the very definition of the political. Everything changed when human activity liberates itself from space; when the mobility of the population and the economy makes nonsense of geographical demarcations. The spatial solidarity of territorial communities is disappearing, to be replaced by temporary interest groups. Now, the nation-state, in its pretension to combine in a unique framework the political, cultural, economic, and military dimensions of power, is prisoner to a spatial conception of power, even as it tries to redistribute its competences according to a federal principle. Space has ceased to be the pertinent criterion. Will politics survive a similar revolution? From the beginning, since the Greek city (polis), politics has been the art of governing a collectivity of people defined by their rootedness in a location, city or nation. If solidarity can no longer be locked into geography, if there is no longer a city, if there is no longer a nation, can there still be politics?

2

THE END OF POLITICS

The disappearance of the nation carries with it the death of politics.

Whichever tradition one is attached to, the political debate presupposes the existence of a body politic. For the French, there can be no expression of sovereignty without the formation of a body politic. For the English and the Germans this is just as indispensable, for it permits citizens to express their "institutional patriotism" in obedience to the laws. But these abstract constructs do not fit well with the reality of modern society: in the age of the networks, the relationship of the citizens to the body politic is in competition with the infinity of connections they establish outside it. So politics, far from being the organizing principle of life in society, appears as a secondary activity, if not an artificial construct poorly suited to the resolution of the practical problems of the modern world.

Once there is no longer a natural place for solidarity and for the general good, the well-ordered hierarchy of a society organized in a pyramid of interlocking powers disappears. There are no longer great decisions from which proceed lesser ones, or laws from which decrees proceed. Just as the community is no longer "contained" in the region, which is no longer "contained" in the nation-state, the lesser decision cannot be deduced from the greater. The crisis of the spatial perception of power is thus felt in the formation of decisions. These, rather than being taken in linear fashion, which locks each entity into a precise competence, are fragmented, and the traditional political debate, a debate about principles and general ideas, an ideological debate, a debate over how society is to be organized, fades away, or rather crumbles, a reflection of the breakup of the decision process itself, and of its professionalization.

Nowhere is this more evident than in the United States. Because it was once in the vanguard of the institutional organization of power, one can see how its institutional logic is exhausted, bringing down with it in its demise politics itself.

In effect, what is Washington today? Dozens of thousands of officials, a few hundred congressmen, several thousand staffers, and, above all else, thirty thousand lobbyists. This last figure does not simply reflect a swollen bureaucracy, but the fundamental upheaval that has intervened in the decision-making process of the greatest modern democracy. "Knowledge is power"—the aphorism holds true, for power lies always in the mastery of information: and in Washington, the treatment of information has undergone a decisive revolution. The days have gone when the job of the lobbyist consisted in knowing several influential senators whom he invited out to lunch, or attempted to corrupt. That approach to the political could threaten the integrity of the democratic process, but it did not call its principles into question. Were a lobbyist to overstep the boundaries, he would be thrown into jail, and morality was saved.

Today, the lobbyist's activities only rarely offend morality, but they undermine the very operation of the democratic machine. Lobbyists deal in information. They mobilize for a corporation or the interests they represent all the information necessary to present the point of view that they have undertaken to defend. If a firm operating in the public works sphere wishes to have funds voted for the construction of a highway, it will gather more complete, precise information than any other public works firm, demonstrating and calculating the advantages of the highway for the community. If, to stay with the same example, the lobbyist represents an association of ecologists, all the deleterious consequences of the project for the environment will be laid out. So, on each case, each law, lobbying firms, lined up against each other, engage in bitter battles in which information is the principal weapon. The offices of the administration are often less well equipped to participate in these confrontations than the different interests present, which have far greater monies at their disposal. Certainly, the lobbyists do not work for nothing, and only interest groups with sufficient funds can engage their services. This is a criticism often leveled at the American system, where only the rich are supposedly able to afford an adequate defense. The criticism is to some extent unfair, since, in the United States, almost all interest groups can muster funds, even the poor, taken as a social grouping. One has only to think of the considerable means that the black community is able to mobilize in its defense.

One might thus optimistically conclude that this professionalization of the craft of lobbyist constitutes a fortunate refinement of a democracy that is henceforth more fully informed. If the confines of a congress are to political ideas what a stock exchange is to shares, can we not establish a parallel in the evolution of these two markets? Just as on the New York Stock Exchange the price of stocks is more and more dependent on the opinion of "institutional" investors, who base their judgment on a professional analysis of company balance sheets, so, in Congress, one might be able to witness a professionalization of debates that are enriched in information of substance by the intervention of lobbying specialists representing opposing interests. Politics can only gain from it.

But is this still politics? The misperception that lobbying fosters is the belief that the general interest will naturally be served by the honest confrontation of special interests.

Now the American system protects private interests very well, and it can even protect public interests as long as they involve a particular group, for example, the charity lobby. However, it is not equipped to plead the cause of a general interest, that is to say, the interest of the entire collectivity as a group. In fact, as the American economy is being internationalized, and foreigners learn their way around the American system, the notion of an American national interest expressed by the Congress of the United States is becoming more and more abstract. By definition, there is no lobby to defend the interests of the "American nation." Such a lobby would, moreover, be very fragile if it were solely the end-product of different interest groups arrayed against each other in Congress. For why should these groups be only American? Korean, Japanese, and European industrialists also resort to the services of lobbyists. If what is good for General Motors is good for America, we will perhaps be hearing one day that what is good for Honda is good for America.

This confrontation thus ends in deadlock, in the absence of a principle of solidarity that would transcend the specific confrontation. The Americans have a metaphor to describe this situation: political gridlock—a political traffic jam. The expression refers to the situation in which automobiles block each other at an intersection: each driver has the impression that the vehicle in front of him is holding him up, although an aerial view would show that each vehicle is in fact contributing to the general blockage. In an advanced democracy, it has become increasingly difficult to raise oneself above particular interests in order to have a bird's-eye view.

This process begins with an unthinking abandonment of the premise of the preeminence of the political: for politics does not exist as a simple outcome of private interests, but presupposes a social contract that precedes it and is greater than all particular contracts. If this premise is abandoned and politics reduced to the function of a market, in which the value of the interests present is up for negotiation, the political space is immediately threatened with extinction, for there is no market that can establish the "value" of the national interest and circumscribe the scope of solidarity. If the national collectivity is no longer a given but a choice, individuals no longer effectively have the means to base this choice on the same rational criteria that guide their actions in the functional management of the national interests. No economic law can replace the territorial and historical basis of the nation.

The professionalization of interests dissolves politics into a multitude of particular confrontations. And if the conscience of a shared destiny, with the memory that this implies, and thus also the capacity to project oneself into the future, remains, here and there, it is not a product of the professionalization of interests, whose logic leads to extreme fragmentation. And in the absence of a regulating principle recognized by everyone as greater than particular interests, the natural tendency is for everyone to pursue his own interests to the furthest extent possible. What could inspire any limits? The best illustration of this is manifest in the litigiousness of American society. To draw up a contract in the United States is always to push for the fullest extent of one's rights, and the lawyers are the soldiers of a society in which all the actors are engaged in headstrong, solitary pursuit of their particular interests. A contract is never more than an armistice in the social battlefield. Beyond the letter of the contract, there is no common ground where, "in good faith," the protagonists could lay down their arms. It is immoral to violate a contract, but there is no morality outside the rules agreed on in the contract. The battle is thus harsh, and often surprises Europeans, who mistake bad faith for a simple absence of faith. It is vital not to leave anything ambiguous, painstakingly to spell out the extent of the rights conceded and obligations contracted. The juridical hand-to-hand combat must not leave any weak spots, for these would inevitably be occupied by the adversary. The duty of an attorney is always to obtain the maximum for any given contract. The other party would not understand it if it were otherwise; and, in certain cases, judges might suspect of collusion and monopoly an enterprise that did not fully exploit all its rights.

There is thus nothing more intolerable than what jurists call a "conflict of interest," the offense of an understanding, because these upset the social machine. If an actor belongs to two spheres of interest at once, the balance of the forces that should foster what is best for society are called into question. It is important that in each act of life, each should obey a one-dimensional logic.

Condorcet and Arrow have shown that it is the only logic that can be compatible with an aggregation of individual preferences. To borrow the jargon of economists, one could say that it is best always to "maximize" utility. The governing principle of this world is not the acknowledgment of a common interest, but the battle of all against all, a confrontation in which each individual's will to power, each locus of power, knows no limit but that of his neighbor's will to power. Each power is exercised to its fullest extent. If this were not the case, power would not be checked, because other powers would immediately occupy the space left vacant by the unnecessary abstention of another power.

In distinguishing clearly between the public and private spheres, the fathers of liberal democracy tried to reconcile the one-dimensional logic of interests with the humanist tradition that makes everyone into a subject: the citizen of modern times had a double life, but, in each of the two facets of this existence, he preserved a certain internal unity. With the abandonment of the premise of the preeminence of the political, this break between public and private does not disappear, but becomes banal, and this banalization pounds to bits the very idea of the subject, which is the other foundation of liberal democracy.

Not only is there nothing that transcends the confrontation of particular interests, but these interests are being fragmented. An individual can simultaneously belong to a political party, a professional union, a consumers' group, and a company; he escapes conflict of interest only when he accepts an infinite division of himself. A constellation of auxiliary professions has appeared, and each one of them—no longer taking care of a particular interest—protects, stages, structures but a facet of this interest. The lobbyist, the lawyer, the banker, the PR consultant, the management consultant, the accountant, each contribute an ephemeral service, a response to a particular situation.

In the end, surrounded by an array of specialists, the modern manager is no longer managing an enterprise but managing situations. It is not surprising that American businesses are criticized for living in the short term. How can there be a memory if there is no subject? The only horizon that counts is that imposed by the quarterly statement. Thus, even taking the long-term view can become a particular function, a specialty, and some enterprises hire "strategy consultants" to determine their goals. This is the ultimate logic of a world that is no longer defined by the human groupings (national or corporate) that it is composed of, but only by the problems with which it must deal.

If there are no particular situations, each situation must be treated on its merits, and not over a period of time, which can confuse calculations and introduces dangerous ambiguities. This is as true for the attorney who establishes a contract without worrying about a climate of confidence between two parties as it is for the banker who negotiates a better purchase price for a company for one of his clients, even if, in the longer term, the industrial value of the acquisition may be cast into doubt. Although the participants in this development may deny it, the American logic puts the stress on the transaction rather than on the relationship with the client, and thus contributes to the fragmentation of a society that manages situations, rather than transcends interests.

The debate, as it loses both in dimension and duration, and as it locks itself into situations rather than organizes itself around principles, is drained of its substance, and it is only by an abuse of language that one can still call it "political." The charge of "mediatization" that is naively leveled at contemporary political life is simply a reflection of a society in which an ephemeral succession of perceptions, as the media choose to stage them, has replaced the consciousness of a common destiny lived in time.

One could even claim that the principal function of the politician, helpless in the face of the gridlock of the professional confrontation of interests, is now the professional management of collective perceptions, and through them the creation of continuity: in the age of the ephemeral, the politician claims to be the priest of the long-term, but uses means that are ephemeral. In this regard, the public figure enjoys clear advantages over the other actors of social life. The mode of politicians' appointment—by election, direct or indirect, through universal suffrage—forces them to tailor themselves to the media and to exist as a media product. The politician thus acquires an original role, as the only human "product" with a general vocation. The other human "products" of the world of the media do not have the same assets: stars of the entertainment world do not generally appeal to more than one segment of public opinion, and are closely linked with a specific product (film, recording, etc.); as for executives, they take care not to obscure the image of their firm.

The politician, in tandem with the television journalist, organizes collective perceptions. The two live off each other, and the ideal—which Ronald Reagan came close to—is realized when the politician no longer has to react to images that cannot be controlled (the tearing down of the Berlin wall, for example), but creates an image, a visual situation that will attract the attention of the media. The objective of the daily agenda is to create situations, in the way a good playwright creates theatrical effects: a sound bite uttered at the right moment, a striking image being more effective than a long message. The high point of a summit meeting is no longer the discussion between chiefs of state but the press conference afterward.

Television imposes its rhythm on the political debate: a good television news program can hardly lead with more than one important subject, and the fear of losing an audience often encourages the executives of different networks to choose the same subject. Only one topic at a time is discussed, and interest soon dissipates: rarely does news coverage spend more than a week on the same question. The politician's task is to play his part as well as he can, to be as often as possible present in the fifty-some psychodramas that fill the television screen each year. These *"tableaux vivants"* have no continuity, something that has both advantages and disadvantages: mistakes, like successes, are soon forgotten.

Fragmentation of images and subjects, the breaking down of time into sound bites, simplification of perceptions: whether something is talked about or not is the principal and often the sole consideration—for an issue that is not talked about does not exist. As for knowing what should be done, this mode of organization of the debate encourages simplistic oppositions. On any given problem, there is a dominant position in relation to which one defines oneself by taking a stand for or against. Nuances and qualifications, the "not exactly" and the "more or less correct" are discredited, because they have no didactic weight. This reveals the handiwork of the lobbyists and the professionalization of information. The enrichment that lobbying affords complicates the process before the fact, and simplifies it after the fact. In the first phases of the making of a law, an extremely tight hand is played out between professionals, who try to fix a given position into the text, far from the political fray. In the final stages—that of public discussion—the professional conflict of interests tends to be neutralized: in almost all cases, there are serious confrontations, at which supporters of the different positions can make their case. Everything at this stage depends on the angle from which a problem is presented. The question of perception becomes crucial, for complexity is tedious, and an argument that cannot be summed up in a single sentence has no media value.

When all is said and done, it is the politician's capacity to impose a particular spin on events that carries the day. President Reagan got some flak for this, even as this former actor's talent for communication permitted some simple ideas to find common currency. True, one cannot relish a situation in which the final decision can be arrived at only by counterfeiting the national debate, which would lead to impasse and blockage. But has there in fact been a decision? Even this is not certain, for the experienced politician knows that nothing is more dangerous than appearances that become reality. In fact, the ultimate stage of democracy by media will be reached when political debate no longer has any influence on actual decisions but on the collective perception that a people has of itself. This perception can be extremely remote from reality. Thus, during the Reagan presidency, and in contradiction to that administration's professed policies, public expenditures increased. No matter: what counted was that the opposite impression prevailed, and that the actors in the economic sphere convinced themselves that in America the state was in retreat. This message, which was heard around the world, had immediate consequences far more important than the budgetary reality. In a contrasting case, it was of little consequence that President Carter had, before President Reagan, started on U.S. rearmament. Carter had not projected the image of a strong president, and his inability to do this counted for more than the reality of the arms buildup.

Here we are then, in all respects very far from the ambitions of the eighteenth century, and from their most advanced expression, parliamentary democracy. The dream of a system of checks and balances, the parceling out of power between several small autonomous poles, creates not equilibrium but paralysis. The public debate illuminated by the light of reason, of which the eighteenth-century philosophers dreamed, is replaced by a professional confrontation of interests.

Liberal democracy rested on two premises, which today are contested: the existence of a political sphere—the locus of social consensus and of the general interest; and the existence of actors endowed with their own energy, exercising their rights, manifesting their "power," even before society constituted them as autonomous subjects. Instead of autonomous subjects, there are only ephemeral situations to deal with, for which temporary alliances can be constructed, supported by competences mobilized for the occasion. Instead of a political space, a locus of collective solidarity, there are only dominant perceptions, as ephemeral as the interests that manipulate them. Simultaneous atomization and homogenization. A society that is infinitely fragmenting itself, without memory or solidarity. A society that finds its unity only in the succession of images of itself that the media feeds it every week. A society without citizens, and thus, in the last analysis, a nonsociety.

This crisis is not, as people in Europe would like to believe in the hope of escaping it, the crisis of one particular model, that of the United States. Certainly, the United States pushes to the limit the logic of the confrontation of interests in which the idea of a general good is dissolved; and the management of collective perceptions in the United States has achieved a degree of sophistication unequaled in Europe. But the extreme case can help to shed light on the average situation, and the American crisis is an indication of our future.

The second country that carries the emblem of our future is Japan, another aspect of the death of politics and the new age of the networks. Japan never knew the constructions of the Age of Enlightenment, the celebration of the individual, the dream of a social clockwork that would respect the multitude of individual destinies. It is passing directly from the feudal age to a modernity in which we do not yet recognize ourselves. Its very success says as much about the end of politics as does the American crisis.

For the success of Japan is not of a political order: in Japan, the professionalization of interest groups and the consequent fragmentation that is a consequence of it actually find a natural counterweight in the memory, sustained by rituals, of a common origin. It thus escapes the gridlock of America, incapable for the time being of reconciling the institutional logic of its origins with the networked logic of contemporary power: paralyzed by negative coalitions, wracked by a multitude of assorted debates that are no longer adjudicated on the common terrain of politics and the general interest. Washington no longer knows how to make decisions. This is not the case in Japan, but it is not politics that saves it from paralysis. It is this country's good fortune to be built on secular customs rather than on a contract. One finds no more citizens in Tokyo than one does in Washington. Japan is not a society but the memory of a society; it mimics power relations. With the same party in power for decades, a charade of democracy is staged there, and the judicious choreography of these carefully limited confrontations is the Asian transposition of the media jousts of modern America. Bunraku in Japan, Punch and Judy in the West: the puppet theater is not the same and does not obey the same rules, but each is equally "apolitical."

From opposing points of departure, each represents the degraded forms of parliamentary democracy, if one understands it as the regime where the executive runs the state under the control of legislative and judiciary branches. In order to have control, these institutional poles of power must continue to exist—although we have already alluded to their disappearance. There must be controllers and controlled. The authors of a decision must be clearly identifiable. This is no longer the case when the multiplication of partners in a decision undermines the traditional vision: the time has gone when a great law established principles, charging the administration with the task of ensuring its implementation. Now there is no more than a succession of small decisions, whose sum constitutes, in appearance more than reality, the "big decision." The American budgetary process, sniped at by the demands of a thousand deadlines and very artificially framed by broad generalities, which constrain nothing but appearances, is an example of a world where the paralysis of institutions ultimately ends in a diffusion of power not so far removed from the Japanese logic. The executive branch has lost the initiative, and the sovereignty of parliament or congress has not been reinforced.

It is thus only to be expected that in the "advanced" democracies the voters vote less, and most politicians have lost the respect of their fellow citizens. Japan, in this respect, as in others, is on the cutting edge of modernity. The politician dreamed of by the Enlightenment philosophers had to be the midwife of a society's truth. Having received the gift of speech at the same time he received that of reason, this politician helped to reveal social transcendence, in parliamentary ceremony. But to entertain such an ambition—the collective and democratic search for the general good—one had to wager that each man is capable of carrying the truth within him, and thus of recognizing it.

Nothing is more foreign to our age than the idea of a person-subject that could exist in and of itself, outside the network of relationships in which it is inscribed and which alone defines it. Of course, we have feelings and even passions that are threatening insofar as they can destroy the homogeneity of the social fabric that facilitates relationships, but these passions do not constitute a person, in the way that sin constitutes a Christian. We are becoming more and more "Japanese," and the visiting card is taking the place both of baptism and the loyalty oath. Like insects tentatively scrutinizing each other with their antennae, we exchange our cards—coded signs essential to the establishment of functional relationship—exclusively defined by the situation that it is the occasion of.

Politeness has thus replaced politics. It is no longer a veneer applied to social reality but the reality itself.

The signs do not refer to any truth that could constitute a common ground on which people can meet. For if that were the case, there would also be the solitary individuals, people hemmed in by their reclusive experience of the truth like Galileo confronting his judges. No, there is no other truth than the social. No longer does the anchorite retreat to the desert. The only knowledge worth cultivating is that of signs—in the attempt to decipher new rules, and not new truths. Knowledge in effect does not consist in discovering some essential truth, but in collecting new signs. It is a search that has no end.

It is commonly alleged that Japan, because it is the most advanced model of a world in which rules replace principles, can simultaneously be impregnated by other civilizations and remain perfectly impermeable to them. It adds signs to its collection of signs. From Europe, it can learn everything, except one thing, the idea of truth. Because it accepts so easily the "truth" of others it does not have to give up its own. For truth, there are only methods, instructions. Any rule that "works" deserves to be taken into consideration.

Having forsaken the project of forming a body politic, caught between the accumulation of signs and the respect for procedure, we industrious atoms of the age of the networks have lost, with the evidence of the nation and of the territory, the foundation of principles that constituted us as a society. The most we can hope for, in imitation of the Japanese, is to find in memory and in rituals the pallid reflection of a society that is no longer.

3

THE LEBANIZATION

OF THE WORLD?

Lebanon suffered fifteen years of massacres, and people had stopped paying attention. For a long time, this was attributed to "the inscrutable Orient," and to a taste for violence ascribed to its inhabitants, a situation that by definition could not threaten the civilized nations. Of course, some people still remember the distant era when Beirut was said to resemble Nice and was the most modern of the capitals of this corner of the world. The only explanation possible was that it was contaminated by an unfavorable environment. And the lesson to be drawn from such a decline was: Let us protect ourselves from these primitive societies that surround us, raise the barriers, cut ourselves off, so that the comfortable complexity of the imperial age is not disturbed by the barbarians by whom we are surrounded. The growing integration of our world of affluence must be accompanied by an increasingly profound break with the world of the poor, which could more aptly be described as "the other world" than as the Third World.

This route, which most do not yet dare to express publicly, is henceforth a hidden temptation of our societies. In Europe, everyone is in agreement in wanting to restrain, and if possible halt, immigration from the South. And without altogether making a principle out of it, we are less closed to immigration from our neighbors to the East, European and Christian, than from those from the so-called South—Arabs, Turks, or Africans, who are for the most part Muslims. Politics, taking its lessons from sociology, now accepts the notion of a "threshold of tolerance," a maximal percentage of immigrants in a given society. Tomorrow, we will admit the principle of a choice between the immigrants from the North and the immigrants from the South. There is a high probability that this choice will be not be made according to the criterion of competence and level of qualification, but according to origin, nationality, and, implicitly, religion. Is the martyrdom of the Muslim community of Bosnia-Herzegovina a sign that there is no place for Muslims in Europe? Will the affirmation of a community's identity be as bloody a process as the conflict of nations was in the past? Immigration to the affluent West and the breakup of multinational states in the East reopen the question of the definition of the community. And in the former Yugoslavia and the former Soviet Union, it is not clear how much violence and fragmentation will have to be unleashed before new solidarities take hold. Lebanon is no longer a country lost somewhere on the map of the Middle East. From now on, it lives in each of us.

The supposed "primitivism" of the Middle East is thus perhaps closer to our modernity than we would like to admit. It shows the dangers of this abstract age, liberated from the constraints of space, into which we are entering. Power does not uncouple itself from space without costs, and the compromise—always fragile—

between the community and the nation is ruptured. Where there is no nation, there is community; where there are no territorial boundaries, there is a search for origins. If you do not define yourself by the place where you live, tell me where you come from.

In the Middle East, it is not space, but water, that is in short supply, and the national grouping has no significance. People group themselves by affinities, in an extended family *(açabiyya)*, a tribe that is attached not to a territory but to chiefs who undertake to protect it, and who often express personal solidarity in a religious light. Saudi Arabia is not a nation. Iraq, by adopting the totalitarian model, is closer to being one: Baghdad was able to create, through war and a police state, the apparatus of a state. But how good is a coerced solidarity? The civil war that has torn Iraq apart illustrates that such a "national" construct is likely not to survive the totalitarian machine that built it.

Is Israel a nation in the European sense of the term? In the beginning, that was the intent: the European Jews who were its founding fathers had a secular vision of the social contract that permitted all sorts of possibilities. As much importance was attached to a certain kind of social relations, to an affinity with the land, as to a specific affiliation.

But once the economic model of the first socialists, the ideal of the kibbutzim, had failed, there was a risk that Jewish identity would no longer be based on a common ideal to be put to work on a chosen territory, but on an affiliation. There would no longer be a nation but a community.

For centuries, this communal logic was viable because it was not in competition with the logic of nationalism. Not only did communities coexist with one another, they were interlinked in a multiplicity of ways. For a long time, the Jews were less persecuted in the Muslim world than they were in the Christian world. Every community had its laws, its representatives, its chief. From the moment that the community pledged allegiance to the dominant power, it was "protected" and enjoyed a fairly extensive autonomy. It bought its tranquillity with a tribute paid regularly to the dominant power, and this limited exchange settled the question of power.

This equilibrium was all the more stable in that expectations on all sides were limited. It was a long way from that age of the nations in which "no one may be ignorant of the law," and in which citizens and nations compose a self-professedly indivisible whole. There was nothing definitive, then, in the divisions between the different communities, despite the religious foundation of these separations. More than once, and in particular in Lebanon—where the communities were more intermixed than elsewhere—it happened that an entire tribe, following the lead of its chief, and for political reasons, would change its affiliation. For a long time, in fact, the relationship to the divinity of the great monotheistic civilizations that shared the Near and Middle East was as pragmatic as their relationship with power. And when compromise was shown to be impossible, nomadism offered another solution: severing the links that bound it temporarily to a territory, a tribe moved on, searching elsewhere for the equilibrium that it could no longer find right there.

Everything started to become more complicated when the East was invaded by some simple ideas from Europe. Power claimed to base its legitimacy on the idea of the nation. And this new ambition led it to want to define territorial limits. The European powers that had managed the Ottoman legacy wanted to map out, with unprecedented precision, frontiers—"imaginary lines in the boundless desert, where the tribes were ceaselessly on the move," as Ibn Saud, king of Arabia, put it. And suddenly, the deserts were crisscrossed with dotted lines, as the abstract logic of Europe erupted into a part of the world where, hitherto, the relationship of the government and the governed had retained a vitality colored by the haggling of the bazaar: eloquent, not exempt from double-dealing, but never totally conflictual, between people who knew they would meet again in a world surrounded by hostile deserts.

The only frontiers had been those that separated the Ottoman empire from its European marches, involving in general a line of fortresses, relatively remote from each other, rather than a precise delimitation. In the interior of the empire, the administrative subdivisions had never defined a real political entity in the European sense of the term. No one would have thought, for a given territory, to calculate the distribution between the different communities. That the Sunnis were in the majority here, the Maronites there, and the Greeks elsewhere, was of little importance. Power did not proceed from the people, and legitimacy was not based on numbers. And even today, most of the states of the region are dictatorships, unrelated to the European idea of democracy. But the principle of national sovereignty has been posed, and its powerful logic is at work everywhere. In the two countries most influenced by European ideas, Lebanon and Israel, there were contradictory consequences, but each proceeds from the same dynamic.

Having failed to define itself as a homogeneous community, Lebanon gradually committed collective suicide. The compromise between the logic of the communal sharing of power and the logic of popular sovereignty did not survive the evolution of the tug-of-war between the different communities, and the country broke up, each of its elements appealing to outside allies. The communities armed themselves, imitating the example of the Palestinian refugees who, in 1969, received from the Lebanese government the permission to maintain armed militias. And to finance their need for arms, they built their own financial organization, supported by all sorts of trafficking, which were developed all the more easily because the state had gradually lost control of the situation. The communities became at once fortress and prison. The dotted lines that had been intended to separate states appeared even within the state itself, isolating villages and even neighborhoods of a single town. Where there was too much intermingling to establish clear boundaries, it took terror to achieve clarity. In the war of the Chouf mountains, the Sunnis, isolated in the Christian-held highlands, were systematically assassinated, and the same fate awaited the Christians marooned in Muslim territory. The map of the communities was thus gradually simplified. The process has not yet played itself out. The Lebanese state remains in an uneasy relationship with Syria, but it is not certain that Syria can dominate Lebanon without jeopardizing its own communal equilibrium, based on the preeminence of the Alawite minority. The infernal machine of Lebanon will thus have repercussions that—throughout Syria, on the one hand, and in the role of the eastern Christians, on the other—will be felt far beyond Lebanon. The massacres in Lebanon tragically illustrate the risks of the communal impulse, which carries within it the crisis of the European idea of the nation.

The creation of Israel was one of the events that precipitated this development. We have seen how the status of Palestinian refugees in Lebanon marked a stage in the logic of "communal-ism" in that country. Paradoxically, the Palestinians, at the outset, scarcely permitted themselves to be locked into the definition of a community: Christian as well as Muslim, the Palestinians defined themselves first of all by the territory on which they were born. It was only after decades of exile that this affiliation gradually took over from the territorial definition. All descendants of Palestin-ians are now Palestinian, as any descendant of a Jew (specifically with a Jewish mother, according to the Hebrew religion) is Jewish.

Contrary to the generous hopes of its mayor, Jerusalem has been divided, instead of unified, and if the presence of a strong Israeli state has ensured that the city not go the way of Beirut, the communal logic that prevails sometimes resembles what has been observed in Lebanon. The same observation obtains for the Arab citizens of Israel: the gulf that has opened up between them and the Jewish citizens of Israel is by no means comparable to the rift that separates the inhabitants of the occupied territories of Israel, but it does not cease to deepen, at the risk of gradually draining of its meaning the principle of the equality of rights that founds a democracy. Israeli Arabs declare their sympathy for states that publicly declare their desire for the destruction of Israel, and Is-raeli Jews discuss the "enemy within." Demographic projections are made, and a "communal" map of Israel is drawn that distin-guishes clearly between Arab and Jewish zones. The electoral pro-cess (proportional, from a national list) handily masks the in-creasingly clear divide between the two "communities," which would seem to promote an electoral process organized on the ba-sis of territorial constituencies. Only a minority talks of expelling the Arabs from the occupied territories, or, a fortiori, the Arabs from Israel, but among sections of Israeli youth, such ideas are gaining currency. As in Lebanon, the question arises of a compromise between communal logic and the logic of national sovereignty. In Israel, the presence of a dominant community helps to avoid the risk that the state will disappear, but not necessarily the risk of its division into communities. There will be no anarchy, Lebanese style, but there may be exclusion along Lebanese lines.

At first, the impossibility of arriving at a territorial compromise between Israelis and Palestinians froze the two sides into a hostile relationship. In a second phase, the deterritorialization of the Palestinian, now defined as the descendant of a Palestinian and a non-Jew of Israel, has led to the search for criteria other than territorial. At this point, Islamic religious identity emerges as the most likely recourse. It is not surprising, then, that support for a movement like Hamas, backed by other Muslim radical groups, has increased. In a third phase, the question of the Palestinian Christians has come up: the logic of communalization will necessarily entail the shattering of Palestinian identity. As in Lebanon, the question of the Christians of the Orient would be posed in tragic fashion if Muslim Palestinians and Christian Palestinians were to turn against each other.

Israel could perhaps extract a temporary security advantage from such a situation. Creating divisions among one's enemies is a traditional strategic goal. But in doing this, Israel would have to lock itself into a communal ideal that would betray the national aspirations of its founders; and if this were the case, the crisis of Israeli democracy would appear not as a particular instance, but as the warning signal of a more general crisis of democratic systems, helpless before the logic of the community. Is this an extreme hypothesis, valid only for the periphery of Europe, the Balkans, abandoned to the fatality of violence?

Perhaps, if one limits the analysis to historical factors: there are in the Balkans, and in a good part of the former Communist world, "communities" that can crystallize all the more rapidly because the nation-states within which they are located have to construct their new legitimacy just at the point in time when the idea of the nation-state is in crisis. But the communal logic that has begun to tear up Central and Eastern Europe is not only the awakening of historical demons that were frozen for a time by totalitarian Communism. It will not necessarily stop at our borders. In other guises, it can take hold in the most advanced democracies, because it also corresponds to the technological evolution of the most modern economies.

How would such an evolution proceed? The intellectual foundations of such an attitude are already in place: one may compare Japan's success with the crisis of America—the triumph of homogeneity and the failure of the melting pot. And there will be no shortage of arguments to advocate this point of view.

Economic evolution effectively requires an increasingly advanced human "integration"—one that excludes everything that is not "normal." The growing formalization of work relationships, indispensable in complex organizations in which computers play an important role, excludes newcomers on two accounts: on the one hand, they must yield to a discipline that is foreign to them; on the other, the formalization of the official structure of power renders the informal structure of power more opaque, even though it is through this channel that evolution occurs— which gives the informal structure a strategic role. The social rules of the game are mapped out more and more minutely, and it is important to be willing to remain in one's place; improvisation is always dangerous. But anyone who believes the key to all the procedures can be found in some manual is mistaken: initiation occurs through a slow impregnation that presupposes the mastery not only of the language but of a whole ensemble of "social signs" that define the community. Although many rules have become implicit, there is no longer, in the modern tribe, a rite of initiation.

Technological development has analogous consequences. The ancient hierarchy of trades, with its innumerable gradations, which created a continuity, from the worker to the engineer, has been simplified, by the disappearance of intermediary levels. Now, on the one hand, there are those who invent knowledge and define the procedures; and on the other, those who carry them out, which, more and more often, means those who supervise their execution by machines. This division into two social blocs, which calls into question the central position of the middle class, the pillar of the moderate republic of recent decades, does not lead back to the nineteenth century and to the class struggle. The individuals in the contemporary enterprise are far too atomized to cultivate bonds of solidarity, far too rootless to find in the notion of social class an answer to their need to belong. Integrated into the enterprise whose regulations they master, but vulnerable nevertheless, solitary, remote from any tangible product, they owe it to themselves to be "conformist"; but this conformity does not afford them an identity.

And what of all those who, in increasing numbers, do not fit into the increasingly rigorous framework imposed by a normalized society? Those who are not "adjusted." Black Americans, North African immigrants. Rejected, cast aside like imperfectly manufactured articles by "quality control"; a control that comes, as in the most primitive factories, at the end of the production line, when school gets out, when it is too late. Instead of swelling the ranks of the middle class, they threaten a middle class that is now uncertain of its identity. A perhaps inevitable counterpart of a world in which homogeneity becomes the key to efficiency, they surround with their disturbing shadow all those precarious little white people who falter in the reckless rush to conform, fleeing before the shadows that are gaining on them.

The sweet warmth of the community, with its one-dimensional simplicity, is thus a very natural temptation. To those who see the idea of the nation becoming more and more abstract, to those who do not participate in the integration of the enterprise, to those that the enterprise isolates, rather than unites, the community is likely to appear as the natural framework within which everyone may rediscover his identity. Without any links to a territory, "nomadic," and nevertheless imprisoned in a function, without an overarching perspective to give a meaning to a given task, modern man, a social nodule infinitely reproduced and nevertheless always single, solitary, is condemned to find difference in a search for origins—a difference that he needs in order to share with others, as different as he is, a feeling of common heritage.

4

AN EMPIRE WITHOUT
AN EMPEROR

The communal impulse appears to be in conflict with the great universal constructs, and if the imperial age is the age of emperors, the era of the diffusion of power—the era of power that cannot be located—is far removed from the era of empires. But if the empire can be distinguished from the republic as the indefinite can be from the definite, as procedure from principle, as the movable from the fixed, the manager from the sovereign, then we are indeed witnessing the eve of the birth of a new empire. An empire whose capital will be neither in Washington, nor in Brussels, nor in Tokyo, nor in Moscow. Rome will no longer be in Rome, and no territorial given, no dominant group, will be able to impose itself. This empire will be neither a supernation nor a universal republic. It will not be governed by an emperor. And yet, it is the concept of empire that most nearly approaches the organization that is emerging. Provided that one bears in mind not the precarious constructs of a Charles V or of a Napoleon, but rather those of the Roman empire, and, perhaps, the Chinese empire, two political spheres whose sovereigns counted for less than the laws that survived them. China was a culture before it was a state. As for Roman citizenship, it was able for several centuries to maintain itself as the dominant political fact, even as imperial power became the subject of sordid political intrigues. An empire without an emperor was possible as long as the barbarians were not at the gates of Rome.

Never have men been as conscious of their number, and never has the idea of the group been more problematic. We no longer believe in the nation, and now the universal republic is being unveiled. Stripped of the certainties of the age of nation-states, when civil society was a given—the legacy on which all sorts of political constructs could be built—we have no convenient formula for defining the scope of our solidarities. There is no legacy today that may not be contested. There is no longer any historical, social or territorial given. The definition of civil society, the delimitation of frontiers, the institution of a political entity have become our choice. In the age of the nation-states, the sole task, for a given group, on a defined territory, was to distribute power equitably; to dispose in its own way the hand it had been dealt. The abstract freedom of the social contract was rooted in a history that, fortunately, limited our choices. Midway between the determinism of the community and the free will of the citizen, the nation offered a convenient compromise. In the postnational age, it is up to us to establish the rules of the game. An onerous responsibility, which would soon become unbearable if it had to obey the laws of classical politics, for there is effectively no political question more difficult to grapple with than that of the definition of the body politic. The debates that this question provokes, whether it is a question of the politics of immigration or of the rights of minorities, clearly reveal, in their intractable violence, our impotence to treat in classical institutional terms the questions facing our age.

In truth, there are no longer any "constituted bodies," and those who expect of the twenty-first century the advent of the universal republic and the realization of Kant's dream are profoundly mistaken. The beautiful pyramid of power, through which the nations would transcend their differences in regional organizations, themselves pillars of a global order, no longer makes any sense. It rests on a model of decision and power that no longer corresponds to reality. The age of complexity is an age of incompletion and of disequilibrium.

We are entering into the age of open systems, whether at the level of states or enterprises, and the criteria of success are diametrically different from those of the institutional age and its closed systems. The value of an organization is no longer measured by the equilibrium that it attempts to establish between its different parts, or by the clarity of its frontiers, but in the number of openings, of points of articulation that it can organize with everything external to it.

The debate over the future of Europe, in its false simplicity, is a good illustration of the inadequacy of an institutional approach in the age of the networks. The dispute between "nationalists" and "federalists" sets up two institutional visions, in which the reflexes of a world that is disappearing reveal how powerless both sides are to take stock of the new world that is taking shape.

On one side, all those who fear for the durability of the idea of the nation are concerned about transfers of sovereignty that threaten national identity and constitute an affront to the dignity of national parliaments. In each country of the European Union, one can find staunch defenders of the idea of the nation—the only framework compatible, in their view, with efficient democratic control, and the only political perspective capable of mobilizing its citizens' energy.

Arrayed against them are all those who, for convenience's sake, one might call federalists. These perhaps have the merit of starting their analysis from the world as it is, and not from an imaginary world that no longer exists, but the Europe that they imagine is as utopian as the nation of the nationalists. They know that, henceforth, the members of the European Union have given up a significant part of their national sovereignty. In the economic sphere, less than 50 percent of existing regulations are now of national origin. One instance of a supranational entity, the European Commission, has become the principal source of regulation, and its sovereignty is henceforth parceled out at several levels—regional, national, and community-wide. In this distribution, certain "federalists" would like to see a replication of the American process, a step on the way toward the United States of Europe and an echo, two hundred years later, of the formation of the United States of America. Superimposing, in a single area, the economic, political, and military dimensions of power, the European Community, for these federalists, will one day have the vocation of becoming a sort of "supernation," complete with its "European identity," as there is an American identity or a French one.

At the moment at which the division between East and West is ceasing to be the organizing principle of the world, this European ambition appears singularly dated. Certainly, the federalists of most consequence justifiably argue that transfers of sovereignty and the extension of the vote to the majority are the only means whereby a European Union enlarged to include from twenty to thirty nations, could still be capable of taking decisions. The European identity of which they dream is not that of the Community of Twelve but in fact that of the historical Europe: to build a political Europe is for them to build a Europe of all the democracies. The institutional model is that of the parallel reinforcement of the powers of the federal executive and of the control of the European Parliament. A coherent construction wholly inspired by the logic of the institutional age.

However, for such an architecture to attract popular support, in order that it become a political project, Europe must remain at the sidelines of the great upheavals of our epoch; it must again become, as it was in the mid-1950s, a sort of democratic island with its frontier demarcated as clearly on the east by the iron curtain as the ocean bounds the United States on both east and west. The European Union could then, as the United States did in the nineteenth century, progressively occupy the field of expansion that history and geography had afforded it. Like the United States of the nineteenth century, it would proclaim its Monroe Doctrine, affirming its own responsibility for the affairs of the Old Continent, from which it would exclude all foreign powers, especially the United States. Such hypotheses no longer correspond to the realities of a networked age, liberated from the constraints, and advantages, of geography.

To the east, there is no longer an enemy in relation to which to define the European democratic exception. It is Europe's fortune and its burden not to let itself be circumscribed by a geographical definition. To the east, Europe has no frontiers, only ill-defined border regions. It abuts on Russia, on the unfinished Soviet landscape. It is impossible for it to claim, in the face of the post-Soviet world, the same otherness behind which it might have the illusion of taking refuge in the face of the Arab world. Confronted with the disintegration of an empire state, Europe is discovering that it cannot, as a federation, become a nation: for that, it would need to define a territory, and thus map a frontier on the east. But how could it establish a frontier that would exclude the country of Tolstoy and Dostoyevsky?

To the west, the Atlantic Ocean offers Europeans the illusion of a more tangible frontier. But that is to grant geography an importance that it no longer has in the age of intangible wealth and the globalization of communication. Not that one can ignore the differences that distinguish Europe from America: the cultural difference, which is most often cited, is not so great, some American universities having become the repository of the best of European culture, and Europe the dumping ground of the worst in American entertainment. More serious are the differences in law—exemplified by the refusal of the U.S. Supreme Court to submit to a superior juridical order, and the differences in political tradition—more "solidarity" in Europe, more "liberty" in the United States. For these differences to be adequate to the founding of a political project, they would have to be powerful enough to capture imaginations and form the "collective perceptions" that, as we have seen, are the only area in which politics today has any purchase.

Nothing is more doubtful, and one can only with difficulty imagine a Europe of tomorrow building an identity by cultivating its difference with America. The European federalists are right to denounce the archaism of the old nationalisms, but wrong to construct a project that in effect posits a European nationalism. Open to the East and to the West, Europe can only constitute itself as a political entity in the manner of the nations that have preceded it: it certainly does not have friends only, but it has no real enemy of its own, only threats to which it and others are subjected. It no longer has the struggles that exhausted, but also formed, the old nations of Europe. For it to become a nation in its turn, it would take a great common misfortune.

It would require that the notion of a "European national interest" have a meaning—whereas, in fact, the very juxtaposition of the terms is enough to illustrate the vanity of the enterprise: The foreign policy of a European Union could not be the simple end-product of the national politics of the individual nations.

There are of course "interests" common to Europeans. The French, the Germans, and the English can hope for the success of the Airbus rather than that of Boeing; they can wish that Europe retain sufficient technological capacities to ensure the prosperity of the continent; they know that the future belongs to those who are capable of training, and holding on to, competence and talent. But this legitimate preoccupation is not enough to define the contours of a new political entity. It can lead to conflicts of interest on certain matters, and collaborations with the United States or Japan on others. It does not found a specifically European identity that would unite Europeans against the outside world on every issue. Such an opposition would, moreover, be profoundly alien to the European tradition. In whose name will Europe speak? The French, who are accustomed to not calling the fact of the national interest into question, will perhaps not even entertain the question. The Germans, wary both of themselves and the politics of power, react very differently: a foreign policy cannot only be the expression of the interests of a nation, even if it is expanded onto the arena of Europe; it must have legitimacy, but what is legitimacy in the age of the networks and the universal empire? Europe defined itself by its ambition of universality, and it cannot abandon this ambition without betraying itself.

The advent of the age of the networks similarly marks the end of politics. A European identity will not be created with a few institutional-age gimmicks. It is not the institutions that create the feeling of belonging; the feeling of belonging makes institutional constraints acceptable. If Washington can no longer manage to reconcile the competing interests of Texans, Californians, and New Yorkers, can one be more optimistic about the reconciliation of Swedes, Poles, Italians, French, Portuguese . . . ? And if we have to have a president elected by universal suffrage in this patchwork Europe, will not the very diversity of its populations increase the chances that Europe will come a few steps closer to the mediatization of public life, taking it still further from its original institutional ideal?

Truly, the confusion of the European debate lies principally in the fact that it is still a political debate over sovereignty—exactly at the point when the Europe of the age of the networks has ceased to be a political idea, which is for the best if it is a question of getting beyond the conflict between nations, and for the worse if one still dreams of free and voluntary citizens.

Europe will not be a rigid institutional structure, settled on a clearly demarcated territory, but an element in an ensemble of competing institutions, obeying no clear architecture and sometimes even escaping all territorial logic, as it is for the principal financial markets, which are increasingly defined by the rules by which they run themselves rather than by geographical location—a location, moreover, that is always an abstraction in the era of electronic transactions. This institutional competition—the consequence of a diffusion of power between several structures that overlap without being superimposed upon each other, which complement each other without being able to eliminate competition entirely—will offer a vanishing political order the mechanisms of power regulation that we can see at work in modern enterprises. The mergers, acquisitions, and takeovers—which in the political sphere would be called wars of conquest, civil wars, partition—will lose their dramatic character only when state sovereignty has fully been broken up into several functional structures. This comes back to saying that Europe will be able simultaneously to manage its internal conflicts and its margins when it has ceased to be a one-dimensional political idea. This is precisely what, in a recent poll, the majority of Germans seemed to be hoping for when they claimed that their ambition for their country was the destiny of a large-scale Switzerland.

This is a prospect that horrifies many of the French, for whom the greatness of a nation is wholly political. As if the death of the political implied the death of Europe. As if Europe could only think of itself as a body politic; as if we were incapable of prospering in the incompleteness of a multidimensional, loosely delimited space. It is precisely this talent that we must acquire, or rediscover, to escape the rigid compartmentalization of the nation-states and reestablish more flexible formulas. Must we seek a response in the earlier stages of European history? The High Middle Ages, with its proliferation of princes, dukes, and bishoprics, was perhaps closer to this model. There is, in the French nostalgia for the political, a strange incapacity to think of values as anything but the expression of a state, as if Montaigne, Voltaire, and Hugo did not owe their greatness to their universality. It is a particularity of the national age to have, for two centuries, sought in politics for the foundation of values.

An imperial age, then, rather than a republican age. One must understand by this not only that the question of the control of power is posed in new terms, but also that the organization of the world is changing in nature. The idea of a universal republic, the legacy of the institutional age, has no sense, because a "body politic" that would come close to the universal would be the very negation of politics, as we have defined it since the word existed. The idea of a universal empire, in the sense in which the Roman empire attained a sort of universality, better describes the reality of the networked world.

The emergence of "postnational" structures in Europe does not in fact result in the organization of the world into three "poles" that, between them, form a sort of board of directors. Europe will no longer be a power in the traditional sense, and no "power" will have all the dimensions of power. Instead we should speak on the global level, of aggregates of networks linked together, like the interlinked rings that are the symbol of the Olympic Games. But, it will be objected, if Europe is not, like the United States, a military superpower, would it not at least have a single monetary currency, a visible attribute of economic power in its traditional form? Beyond the fact that the central bank would take care, in order to ensure its credibility, to set itself at a distance from the traditional forms of political power, there is every reason to imagine that the lifespan of an "independent" European currency would be very brief. Because of the importance of the market that it will serve, a European currency would in fact be a highly credible alternative to the dollar, which will create a high risk of markets becoming volatile, floating capital being susceptible to migrating abruptly from one currency to the next, in response to the economic news of the day. There is no doubt that the need for coordination, which already exists between the dollar and other currencies, will become an imperative necessity. And as one can already see, the stabilization of exchange rates requires a coordination of monetary policies that, in the long run, is viable only if it is accompanied by a harmonization of budgetary policies. A European currency thus logically leads to a global monetary system, a transposition hierarchically similar to that of the OECD countries of the European Monetary System. Such a global system would lead to a single currency and a "unified economic space" regrouping the richest parts of the world, and would become in this fashion not homogeneous but "interlinked" (in other words, standardized, in the sense that munitions or broadcasting systems are).

This multidimensional world, in which no structure can monopolize all the dimensions of sovereignty, favors openness, in contradistinction to the closed system that is embryonic in all political logic. In this way, as the questions at issue acquire a universal dimension, whether it is a question of drugs, of the environment, or of financial matters, it becomes increasingly absurd to want to resolve them within the same framework. Geographical expansion requires functional specialization, and any attempt at political totalization, whether European or not, appears as an artificial relic of a bygone age.

The postnational age into which we are entering can also be qualified as imperial insofar as, like the Roman empire, its "frontier" is no longer a line that divides a space and separates men— those who exercise sovereignty and those who do not—but rather as an uncertain margin. The plenitude of one sovereignty does not, as in the era of the nation-states, butt up against the plenitude of another sovereignty on the other bank of the river. The same movement that tends to relativize frontiers within the European Union will relativize the frontiers of the community itself. No frontier will be absolute.

Like the Roman citizen of the time of Caracalla, the citizen of the imperial age of the networks defines himself less and less by his participation in the exercise of sovereignty and more and more by the possibility he has to act in a framework in which the procedures obey clear and predictable rules. These vary, from Tokyo to Washington or Paris. There is a specific geography for each function, for each problem, and the juridical competences may thus not have the same reach, but compatibility is the rule. This slippage of law, formerly the expression of the one-dimensional sovereignty of a political body, today a simple operating procedure governing a functional base of sectors of human activity, ruins the autonomy of the political, which loses its moral and philosophical foundations. It becomes effectively just as incongruous to pose the question of legitimacy as to question whether a computer program is "just" or "unjust." The gentle whirr of the social machine is sufficient unto itself.

Little by little, this transformation will reduce to the same level rules emanating from processes that are still provisionally called political and those that result from the concerted action of enterprises. It matters little whether a norm is imposed by a private enterprise or by a committee of bureaucrats. It is no longer the expression of a sovereignty but simply something that reduces uncertainties, a means of lowering the cost of transactions, of increasing transparence.

This "networked" logic continually calls into question the frontiers of legal jurisdictions: To facilitate transactions in a given space it should not complicate them once one crosses the limits of this space.

The profit accrued in internal transactions should not be wiped out by any eventual extra costs of external transactions. The logic of the world of the networks thus leads to the universal norm, to the increasingly efficient connection of network nexuses.

In the past, parliaments that declared themselves to be sovereign would vote on a customs tariff that applied to goods crossing a frontier. Today, "services"—these immaterial products of the age of the networks—derive their development from exchanges. Now, precisely because they are immaterial, their increase is no longer linked to the lowering of a customs tariff—they never physically cross a frontier—but to the harmonization of internal regulations, so that a bank or an insurance company can install itself in the country of its choice, there to develop the connections from which it creates wealth. The debates of a sovereign parliament have been superseded by a negotiation between bureaucrats, who are accountable to no parliament, because no parliament can modify a detail without bringing the whole structure down. We are far from the universal republic. What is coming into being is not a global political body but an apparently seamless fabric, an indefinite accretion of interdependent elements.

This is the logic of the networked world, but not yet its reality. The space of the networks is in fact neither neutral nor homogeneous. It is a field of forces, of imbalances, in which the will to increase the number of one's connections is counterbalanced by the fear of losing control of the networks that have already been set up. This tension is at the heart of the dynamic of our societies: the world is becoming a gigantic stock exchange of information that never closes. The more information there is, the more imbalances there are: as in a great meteorological system, a wind that creates a depression here, causes high pressure elsewhere.

Our "political" institutions, because they are still largely inspired by an institutional logic, do not know how to handle this tension between a dynamic openness and a protective isolation. The definition of frontiers, the constitution of a body politic are still understood as essential, the stable foundation on which a society may subsequently be constructed. The logic of the networks will completely upset this perspective: the frontier is no longer a beginning, but an ending, always precarious, by nature fluid—for fluidity becomes the condition of competition and of dynamism in the age of the networks. No juridical space is ever definitively fixed.

This can be seen already in the functioning of the multinational corporation, the symbol of this new world. Neither enclosed in the customs of a native land nor abstractly stateless, the transnational enterprise builds its success on the quality of the relational "links" that it has established. It no longer sets its sights on being a giant in an economy of scale but on a perfect circulation of information, which makes it into a hypersensitive seismograph, continually animated by the innumerable impulses that its receptors register from the outside world: new products, new financial instruments, new manufacturing processes.

Each unit of the enterprise must be sufficiently grounded in its local network fully to play its role of receptor vis-à-vis the "outside" and be sufficiently "linked" to the other units of the enterprise to act out fully its role as distributor within the company.

Transparency, circulation of information, clarity in defining tasks—these are the conditions for the smooth functioning of a complex structure, and facilitate the emergence of a corporate identity that mobilizes its employees around a common ambition. But from a dynamic perspective, these advantages can become dangers: too distinct an identity can stifle new ideas; organizational structure, too well defined, can foster passivity, if not irresponsibility, when each employee's margin for initiative is limited to the narrow task that has been entrusted to him. A certain dose of unsettling ambiguity is necessary to maintain the dynamism of the enterprise. And the different actors of the entrepreneurial game, submerged in the increasingly abundant flow of information, must never be completely assured of the place that they are assigned to—of what their role is. The circulation of information cannot result in the institutionalization of transmitters and receivers of information. Information thus remains the basis of power, but its nature has changed: it can no longer be hoarded, and its value is entirely in exchange. The primary goal of information is to acquire more information.

The same choices between transparency and secrecy, between relational fluidity and institutional stability, can be observed in the relationship between the corporation and its environment.

The enterprise in effect tries to withhold information, to maintain an advantage over its competitors, but since it has itself to secure a maximum of information to be competitive, it is encouraged to multiply "relationships" and "connections," and each relation "betrays" it a little. It must thus continually choose between a secret that protects it and an instructive openness to the outside, between the defensive and the offensive in the battle for information.

As soon as the frontier is no longer a given, whether in the case of a corporation or a state, the function of management, and thus the nature of power, changes.

The managers thus become "intermediaries" rather than bosses, constantly adjusting the organization of the relationships between thc different units. To direct a transnational enterprise is to manage the dynamic tension between the function of "receptor," tuned to external networks, and that of "transmitter," tuned in to the internal network of the enterprise.

And even this management is efficient only if it is strongly decentralized. For the functioning of the enterprise has its "frontiers." The definition of its relationships with its suppliers and its customers requires a multitude of microdecisions—for example, on the definition of computer interfaces—which cannot originate from the management. And if too strong a contradiction appears between the strategic logic as laid down by those at the top and the "networked" administration on the periphery of the corporation, this is generally resolved by a redefinition of strategy, or by a crisis that brutally modifies the shape of the enterprise; for example, the decision of a group of executives who decide to pursue clients (or suppliers) independently, in opposition to the company's overall strategy. The strategic and organizational vision of the directors of the corporation is thus constantly competing with the de facto arrangements operating, the new circuits developing on the periphery of the enterprise, and in response to the networked impulses of which it is the object.

To respond to this new situation, the internal structure of the enterprise changes: the hierarchical pyramid tends to disappear.

The "natural" model, with straightforward, spreading branches, is succeeded by the multidimensional model, based on so-called interlocking databases. The hierarchical, pyramidal structure, in which to be powerful was to control and command, is succeeded by a structure of diffusion of power, with multiple connections, in which to be powerful is to be in contact, in communication, and in which power is defined by influence and no longer by mastery. This new organization becomes possible thanks to techniques of communication that permit a far more flexible management of information.

The number of hierarchical levels is reduced, and the hierarchy of salaries no longer corresponds to that of function. The president of a company is often not as highly remunerated as some of his collaborators. A bizarre anomaly due to an imbalance in the job market? Not at all. Rather, an acknowledgment of the value of the networkers, who, through their contacts, create the wealth of the enterprise.

Consultants, brokers, lawyers, investment advisers, "head hunters," all of them first and foremost professionals, working for the most part outside the large corporation—a lingering relic of the institutional world—these are the symbols of the age of the networks into which we are entering. Not only do they avoid the institutional red tape that paralyzes large organizations, but they permit the large organization to be bypassed, by offering entities of a more modest scale technical expertise and specialization that they could not independently acquire. This is the ultimate phase in an "institutional competition" that gives the enterprise the maximum flexibility: not only is the shape of its activities unceasingly modified by the play of its mergers and takeovers, but it becomes possible to manage certain operations, formerly considered strategic, in the form of services, by resorting to competences outside the enterprise. Ultimately, the management of the enterprise no longer needs to consist of more than a few people capable of selecting, then managing, the professionals outside the operation whose services it is hiring on a temporary basis. Power no longer consists in knowledge, but in functioning as a link between bodies of knowledge.

The logic of such a system will force the large corporation to accept profound changes. The monoliths and economies of scale of the industrial age count for less than the capacity to invent new modes of relationship, which will turn the client or the supplier into partners rather than strangers or competitors. Enterprises of a moderate size will emerge by fission, for in an economy in which value is derived more from a transaction than production, groups come together or break up as a function of their capacity to lower the costs of transaction, in an economy constantly readjusted between the logic of homogenization of relational nexuses and the logic of differentiation. For as soon as the organization into networks prevails over the pyramid structures of the institutional age, as soon as there is no longer a "center," one of the principal justifications for the large organization falls by the wayside. The point is no longer to impose a common direction from above, but, more subtly, to manage identities and ensure the compatibility of these identities with other identities. The logic of the networks, which implies the multiplication and thus the decentralization of connections, suggests that the optimal size for managing these identities is much smaller than that of the great enterprises of the industrial age.

In the domain that is still described as political, such a fact will have decisive consequences. It will no longer be a question of concentrating more and more power in ever-larger political entities, but only of organizing compatibility, preparing for convergence, by establishing procedures for the manufacture of rules, more than in building sovereignties. We have shown what this new logic signifies for Europe. We will see it for the vast, indeterminate space that is Russia. Could Russia perhaps pass directly from the prenational empire, imposed by force from the center, to the postnational empire, a network of agreements facilitating the compatibility between open units, rather than the architecture artificially built around a capital? The chaos in the former Soviet Union, and the extreme violence to which it may lead, is a good illustration of the limits of institutional logic. All attempts to define a geography of sovereignties, which would be enclosed in a system all the more precise for being more absolute, is destined to violence, and it is very unlikely that a federal pyramid of interlocking powers can bring a stable institutional response. More likely is the coexistence of new feudal powers that, in the heterogeneous immensity of the Soviet territory, may perhaps prepare the entry of the Russian world into the world of the networks. For this, the Russian nation must skip the phase of the nation-state and its conflicts and pass, like Japan, directly from the feudal age into postpolitical modernity.

The imperial age that is beginning will thus only on the surface be a period of large organizations. These, having undergone the apprenticeship of complexity and multiple identities, in accepting that their frontiers resemble more the uncertain limits of the Roman *limes* than the precise lines of the age of nations, will prepare the advent of an eminently fluid world, whose stability will no longer rest on institutions but on a mode of diffusion of change—the capillary-like network of microdecisions that will prevent ruptures as much as it will prevent immobility. This world will be all the more stable for being more flexible, a world that should be thought of in biological schemata, rather than those of physics. It will be a world of rules, rather than of principles.

5

INVISIBLE CHAINS

What is liberty in a world of rules? How can power be limited in a world without principles?

For two centuries, we have associated the idea of democracy with that of liberty. But liberty has two very different senses: it has been the right of a human collectivity to take its destiny in hand, and thus to endow itself with a government that would express its collective will; it is also the right of each individual to be protected from abuses of power—the guarantee that the minority will not be crushed by the majority.

With the advent of the imperial age, it is clear that the first conception of liberty is moribund and that the imperial age promises us, at best, the limitation of power. The process of concentration of power begun several centuries ago has ended, and with it the parallel effort to control, in an institutional equilibrium, the exercise of power. The idea of the sovereign has lost its force of attraction, and with it the idea of a sovereign political body. In a way, we should perhaps rejoice in this, insofar as liberty that is an exercise of the general will posed a threat to liberty—liberty as the right of the minority. Those who effectively exercised power abused it all the more in that they claimed to exercise it in the name of all the people. From this point of view, the advent of the "state of law," the designated successor of democracy, unsettled by the imperial age, would seem to promise us liberty far more surely than a democratic age in which universal suffrage conferred a formidable legitimacy on an unprecedented concentration of political power. There is, however, some naïveté in imagining that the liberty of the relational age, the liberty of the age of conformity and of corruption (see, in particular, chapters 6 and 8), will have the same quality as the liberty that inspired Galileo or Montesquieu. *Liberty* is a word of the institutional age: will the word still have meaning in the imperial age?

We have already shown how the classical conception of parliamentary democracy was progressively destroyed by the disappearance of politics, the locus of general ideas and grand decisions. The crisis of the mechanisms of institutional control do not, however, signify that there is no longer any control at all. But the controls of the imperial age confer a new meaning on the word *liberty*.

In the age of microdecisions and of the confrontation of special interests, only choices with regard to individuals can in fact still give the illusion of liberty, and thus of the possibility of control. Questions regarding individuals henceforth prevail over questions of principle. One can see this well in the United States, where the high points of "political" life are the moments at which a half-parliamentary, half-judiciary procedure puts a public official in the hot seat. But what a strange control!

Debate over a problem transforms itself into a debate over the personal integrity of an individual, over his respect for institutional norms, the last criterion of judgment in a world in which the political game has no other object than the preservation of the rules of the game, the only agreed operating standard of a society without a goal. No accounting is demanded of a policy, only the assurance that a procedure has been respected—these procedures that are supposed to permit the control of the legislative over the executive. Everyone knows that this control no longer makes much sense. It is in fact replaced by a purely formal charade of coherence, a sort of parlor game, which, as in a medieval ordeal, presents in the forum of public opinion, rather than before ecclesiastical judges, the actors of public life. And the emotion that the televised broadcast of a hearing evokes creates the collective perception that society needs to continue to think of itself as a society. A justice of the United States Supreme Court is not asked to embody a vision of the law, but that he offer a "snapshot" of a society as it imagines itself. The principles of law and ethics are not debated—on the contrary, the judge being questioned attempts to demonstrate that he has no opinion about anything. We only contrast one snapshot with another. Thus, the debate on the confirmation of the nomination of Judge Clarence Thomas to the Supreme Court contrasted the edifying image of the little black boy climbing the social ladder with the repellent image of the seducer who tries to abuse his coworker.

Theatrical as it is, this staging of transparence is in itself an obstacle to the development of power, and no one will contest that the multiplication of procedures and rules is a powerful brake on the arbitrary. But, as can be seen from the evolution of the U.S. Supreme Court, the proliferation of rules at the very point that principles are in demise is now as much the expression of the need for a social ritual as of the concern to protect "liberty." And these "liberty brokers" that lawyers claim to be are above all the priests of a new ritual. They organize and certify conformity more than they limit power.

In fact, in step with the progress of the imperial age, the role of the lawyer is changing: rather than being a manager of conflicts, he becomes an engineer of relationships, and this transformation is upsetting commonly perceived notions of liberty.

The institutional age multiplied the choices available, and thus the occasions for experimenting with liberty: political choices, but also the choice between public and private life. The imperial age has a horror of choices, and if it limits power, it is not by organizing conflict, but by parceling out decisions.

It is in fact much better suited to preventing conflicts than to resolving them. In the imperial age, conflict becomes a social anomaly. In a world that is well "connected," with transparent rules, conflict supposes an incomprehensible incompatibility of perceptions: if there are both weak and powerful, how dare the weak engage in battle, when their defeat is inscribed in the social order? Either the hierarchy of society must have been profoundly disturbed, or, from one sector of society to the other, people can no longer be reasoning in the same way—homogeneity must have been lost. When society is functioning, there is no time for conflict to appear, it is dissolved in a multitude of microdecisions and microadjustments, in which the weak test the strength of the strong, and the strong make the weak feel the force of their strength, and in which everyone, in the last analysis, finds their place. We are thus also as far here from the institutional age of power, which institutionalizes conflict, as from the feudal age, in which the triumph of the strong leads to the absorption of the weak. In the imperial age, the strong are sufficiently strong as soon as the weak have come to recognize their place. A certain social geography naturally imposes itself.

This peaceful tranquillity of the imperial age is not that of the triumph of reason. It covers the muffled echoes of the thousand little piecemeal battles that have prepared the way for the splitting off of great confrontations. In this respect, Japan is much more "modern" than litigious America.

Decision making in Japan takes much longer than in America, and its implementation is shorter. The differences are the result of contrasting approaches to the decision-making process. During the period that precedes the decision, the Japanese firm has many meetings in which the expression of many points of view is encouraged. These can be expressed with all the more candor in that they at no point call into question the strict hierarchy of the enterprise: a hierarchy that includes far fewer echelons than a European corporation, and in which advancement occurs in large part through seniority. In contrast to the European or American enterprise, in which what is at stake in the meeting will also be a battle between individuals—the person who can make his point of view prevail will at the same time advance his career—the two spheres here are perfectly distinct. The very rigidity of the hierarchy of the enterprise authorizes the brutality of discussion. But the intent in having so many meetings is in fact not to come to a hypothetical consensus—a myth that underestimates the brutality of hierarchical relationships in Japan. The decision will be made by the most senior member of the hierarchy, perhaps in contradiction with the points of view expressed in the course of discussion, but after debates that will in some sense have "polished," by friction, the different opinions offered. Like a marble that ricochets from obstacle to obstacle, the decision will have been enriched by the exchange of information, and if it falls to the chief to draw conclusions from the discussion, his intervention is only the ultimate sanction of a process that has diffused power.

The final decision can only conclude a long series of microdecisions, and all those who have had the honor to contribute to the discussion can henceforth bear a part of the responsibility they share. In the course of the debates, after having thrown out unorthodox opinions, perhaps brutally, they have been able to observe the effect produced, and to adjust their attitude to correspond with their hierarchical position. A process of self-limitation has been worked through. The deliberative councils typical of Japanese society thus have a dual role: they link those who are to put it into effect with the decision, and they mime the social theater, permitting the decision makers to test, in a game of reciprocal checks and balances, the limits of their power. A power that is not bound by any supposed obligation to take the opinion of subordinates into account, and, more subtly, by a concern not to weaken their power by abusing it.

Japan is, from this point of view, the exact opposite of the United States: in a situation where the American logic pushes everyone to the furthest limit of his possibilities, in a struggle arbitrated by the law of the social contract, the Japanese logic counsels moderation and prudence. If there is no law that allows conflicts to be arbitrated, no transcendence that makes it possible to say where the truth is, no power that can check power, it is vital, if society is not to tear itself violently apart, that power restrain itself. The "tyranny of little decisions"—to use the formula of Jean Padioleau, a subtle analyst of organizations—replaces the arbitrary by strategic pseudochoices.

In such a decision-making process, there is no center or supreme power, only a multitude of groups that are trying to increase their power without going so far as to attack the power of neighboring groups. Each one tries, in a complex game of self-limitation and interdependence, to prevent a partner from taking a dominant position. Japanese capitalism, with its groups of enterprises, *gurupu*, of the more integrated *zaibatsu* of the prewar period, illustrates well the mixture of fierce competition and forced compromise that characterizes the Japanese business world. Between 60 percent and 70 percent of the shares of Japanese companies are held through joint partnerships, which ensures the solidity of the groups, sheltering them from all hostile action, and imposing compromise. The optimal situation is that in which all the elements of society have been integrated in a game of reciprocal dependencies. No longer are there any subjects, but an extreme diffusion of power, multiplied, rather than fragmented.

The diffusion of power has taken the sting out of conflict. And like a block of granite that is being eroded into sand, the imperial age is dissolving conflicts into a thousand impalpable fragments. Social stability is the stronger for it, but the clarity of debate is losing out. This form of limitation of power is not the triumph of liberty. The self-limitation that is its foundation is not produced by the system, for the system produces only rules, never principles. That is why if, by misfortune, this process of dilution has not taken place, confrontation easily becomes unmanageable: the procedural formalism that increasingly characterizes our societies is tolerated only if it is applied to decisions of limited impact. From the moment that power is limited, not by virtue of an overarching principle but through fidelity to a collection of behaviors whose memory it guards, and that it is responsible for passing on because they have functioned before and will do so again, the mechanism of self-limitation is threatened. Let a fundamental question appear, a question of principle, and the formality of the rule reveals its utter fragility. The attenuated network of procedure on which the imperial world is built can resist tensions only if the diffusion of power has been pushed to the limit. If a strong pressure is brought to bear at any point on this fragile fabric, the fabric is immediately ripped apart. Thus, sometimes our liberty is locked into a multitude of little decisions and appears totally insignificant; at other times it is confronted with a major decision and then cannot act, for want of a political framework robust enough to resolve conflicts.

Thus it is no surprise that this liberty, able to express itself only in the derisory, contributes to the discrediting of politics: politics, in losing its autonomy, has lost the capacity to produce true decisions. The imperial age does not rate very high in its scale of priorities the need for a society to be composed of free men. It is not that, like the dictatorships of the institutional age, it makes a great effort to stifle liberty; only that it has given up making it its principal ambition. But is this still of any importance to the people of today? Plunged into a deep slumber, they are like Gulliver in Lilliput: bound not by heavy chains, but by a thousand little cords so slender that they are almost invisible, to the point where only the rare individuals who still have the memory of another age can sense its powerful presence.

The great surprise of this age is that most of us feel comfortable with it. We have the feeling that we have never been as "free," and we pity our forefathers, who were subjected to all kinds of constraints that no longer bind us. Whether it is a question of the movies we watch, the clothes we wear, or, more important, the feelings we experience, there are almost no taboos left. Why does this liberty leave a taste of ashes in the mouth? What are we so attached to?

6

THE NEED FOR CONFORMITY

The age that we are leaving behind, the age of institutions and politics, recognizes difference but organizes it and frames it. It distinguishes and separates those who decide from those who obey; those who legislate from those who judge; and so on. It organizes conflict in order to transcend it. The imperial age does not tolerate conflict, which it calls misunderstanding. It needs similarity. In place of a structural hierarchy, it offers the benefits of teamwork. Instead of polarity of power, it prefers an ever more advanced circulation of information, the object of which is to dissolve conflict by a multitude of precautionary microadjustments.

The age of politics implicitly reproduces a mechanistic model of behavior, in conformity with a linear vision of power: in this model, we must have great causes to produce great effects, and great powers to conduct great policies. The age of the networks has no such ambitions. In a century that has known two world wars, a century in which catastrophe theory was invented, it knows that strength is not a linear function of power and that, from small causes, can come great effects.

If one were to borrow a model from the exact sciences, it would thus be that of meteorology, that of a perfectly rational yet nevertheless unpredictable world, in which the infinitesimal modification of one variable can provoke a fundamental rupture; a world that defies the observer and the progress of observation to the extent that the pertinence of a variation has no bearing on its importance. This means that the ambition to control the system, and the equation of the political official with some great social clockmaker presiding over the heart of the inner workings and regulating the whole machine within the confines of an equilibrium of controlled forces—the "escapement" that clockmakers invented in the eighteenth century—these no longer make any sense. The political sphere is no more susceptible to control than the weather. One must thus approach the question of the organization of societies with far more modesty and prudence, and in what one might call a peripheral fashion, since there is no institutional center.

To pursue the meteorological image, one could say that storms—for example, cyclones—arise precisely out of the unpredictable, and always unstable, encounter of two masses of air of different characteristics. The same goes for the social sphere, in which the problem is first and foremost to manage differences, in which many invisible microadjustments must be made to avoid great traumatic shifts. The ideal of this world is not institutional conflict but an "anticyclonic" calm that nothing could upset; a stable state in which homogeneity is the rule and difference the anomaly.

Japan, until the recent past, offered the best approximation of this ideal. The most finished attempt to implement a "networked" conception of power, the diffusion of information that can be observed there is yet more efficient because it permeates a homogeneous society: the information is not distorted by a dangerous differentiation of social elements that it traverses and whose function is to carry it along. There are no—and neither should there be—particular "points of view"; there are only a multitude of adjustments that are in fact just so much information, and which together make up the increasingly abstract notion that is still called power, but which is no longer the prerogative of a determined subject. In this world, power no longer resides in a prince capable of imposing his will on the social entity, but in the social entity itself; and the power of the social entity is not the appropriation by the collectivity of the powers of the prince— that was the illusion of the institutional age—but its capacity to exist as a social entity and not as a political body. It is a question of conveying information in all directions and, in so doing, to exist like a huge cybernetic machine.

The smooth operation of the machine does not demand philosopher-kings, or enlightened citizens, but "equals," interchangeable elements capable of interlocking efficiently with one another in innumerable combinations. The variety of the possible relationships condemns the actors of the social game to homogeneity, to standardization. These, like the pieces of a Lego set, can be connected to each other in the most diverse combinations. To use another image, one can compare society to a vast brain, in which the connections between neurons are made thanks to billions of electric impulses that circulate all the more fluently as long as the neurons bathe in a perfectly homogeneous medium. In a society in which power is a function of the networks, social "conductivity" becomes essential.

The Christian tradition has taught us that each man carries within him an interior source that constitutes him as a subject, and authorizes him to judge the world, that each man is a consciousness, and that this consciousness is irreducible. It is this ego that we are called upon to give up. Not for the benefit of a social will supposed to be superior to it—that is the illusion of authoritarian regimes—but to subject us all the more completely to our external interface. Descartes's subject could declare: "I think, therefore I am." The "equal" of the age of the networks could say: "I communicate, therefore I am." The "equal" is not interesting in itself, nor in reference to a social entity that is supposed to be the bearer of its own meaning. There is thus no hidden meaning in society to be deciphered, but only a programming of social particles that permits them to connect with one another, to work with each other. If this principle of manufacturing were more than a sign, if there were a message to decipher, society would have to call in decryptors, and thus reintroduce the subject. Kafka, describing the dawn of the imperial age, suggests in *The Great Wall of China* that there are still laws, but that these laws are secret, illegible to those obliged to respect them. Roland Barthes, in *Empire of Signs*, has a more serene feeling for the mythical Japan that inspires his reflections. There is no signified beyond the signifier, and that is just as well. It is up to us to make our own way as best we can through the grammar of signs.

In a society without a goal and without a meaning, the "social message" is thus reduced to the idea of a connection, and the connection is all the more efficient in that it is perfectly empty of meaning, infinitely reinterpretable. The network, which the Chinese call *guanxi* and which for them is an essential element of the social game, prevails over the individual.

This means of regulating the behavior of a society is so alien to our traditions that we have only pejorative terms with which to

describe it—so pejorative that they seem vulgar to those specialists who fear to appear less intelligent by being less subtle. The
word *conformity*, like the word *corruption*, is in the process of becoming archaic. However—and the Japanese model helps to ex-
plain this development—the imperial age imposes a generalized
supraconductivity that no longer leaves room for individual differences. Conformity is not an accident, a regrettable weakness of
advanced industrial societies, but a necessary condition of their
smooth operation.

By conformity, one must understand not the blind pursuit of
the center by the periphery, but rather that capacity, proper to
"modern" man, of avoiding dissonance. Traditional conformity
implies a subordination to a dominant class that imposes its ways
of thinking on the rest of society: it provokes nonconformity, a
reaction against the ideology of the moment and an individualis-
tic affirmation of liberty.

The new conformity is less easily graspable and on the surface
more tolerant: nonconformity is no longer a threat to it. On the
contrary, because of the impetus it gives to the social machine,
nonconformity has its usefulness. But it does not know how to
exist, exactly to the extent that it does not encounter real resistance, for every new reaction against conformity is no more than
the germ of a new conformity, and merits consideration on these
grounds. By its very existence, nonconformity modifies the social
geography and transforms conformity. Strictly speaking, just as
there is no longer any polarization of power, there are no longer
opposing poles of conformity and nonconformity. There is only
an endless race for uniformity, because as the runners move for-
ward, it transforms the image that they are pursuing.

So, as in a large meteorological system, the behavior of each social molecule can be explained at any given instant, but the formation of destabilizing imbalances, because it is not determined by big causes, evades explanation and prediction. This is why the iconoclast, the professional disruptor, has a place in such a system. His role is to shake things up without threatening anything. Strictly speaking, no longer are there leaders of opinion, only individuals or organizations that, with the right touch applied at the right moment, in the right place, keep ahead of conformity. So an Italian fashion designer, thanks to a computer system designed to pick up information rapidly from numerous retail outlets, will know before his competitors that mauve is the color of the summer and puffed sleeves the style of the moment. He will take the consequences of this into account for his next collection, which, in its turn, will create ripples that will make fashion evolve. A slight innovation, built on fragile commercial observations, can have important consequences on winter fashions. And these repercussions themselves still further amplify, beyond all expectations, the effect of the first success. Once critical mass is reached, a chain reaction sets in.

The same phenomena can be observed in what remains of what used to be called the world of ideas. There is a particular category of books whose authors just happen to act as "social barometers." They felicitously express the intellectual disequilibrium of the moment, throwing ideas into the spotlight, just as politicians throw the spotlight on the social debate. An important function, permitting the social group to keep in touch, simultaneously posing the identical questions of the moment, concurrently, questioning themselves on the how, while scrupulously avoiding the why. No matter that these successive interrogations are contradictory, no matter that, as events unfold, observable realities rapidly give the lie to them. They repose not on the principle of truth, but on that of resonance. And just as a high note, however faint, can shatter a crystal glass if it is of the right frequency, a book can resonate with society. And it may happen that because of this resonance, ancient traditions that had been imagined to be eternal can shatter. From small causes, great effects.

The imperial age is thus an age of mirrors. It is a play of reflections, a pale world, stalked at once by precariousness and by boredom, navigating between storms and utter calm, needing the imbalances without which no wind can come up, but fearing the unforeseeable ruptures that every disequilibrium threatens. And the very volatility of a world in which all the elements are holding each other in place, and which a mere nothing can set in vibration, is at the heart of modern angst.

Virtually no one dares declare himself "conservative" today, for no one feels assured enough of the principles worth preserving. Meanwhile, everyone recognizes that change is the rule of the imperial age, its driving force—but equally, everyone admits that "change" is beyond human control. Whether at the level of enterprises or of nations, everyone is now careful not to claim to plan for the future, contenting themselves with developing their "capacity to adapt." Adaptability has in fact become an essential value, and a modern manager is judged by his flexibility: that he is able to find his feet in a new setting, that he can forget "old" ways of thinking, is a promise of success. The manager is first of all required to be accepted by the team; his integration into the professional milieu is a matter to be evaluated, and any idiosyncrasy that might weaken the organization becomes a cause for concern.

It is no surprise then that contemporary success is fraught with uneasiness, not to say angst: the anxiety of not being "dynamic" enough, "optimistic" enough, upbeat enough. It is the angst of being an empty mold, social modeling clay, living in the eyes of one's colleagues and superiors. The company man may scarcely permit himself to have principles: he must have reflexes. A man of few convictions, it would be bad form for him to appear cynical. He is expected to administer his interior emptiness with alacrity. A man of little meaning, he must, in the world of signs without significance, become a cipher himself. And it will be appreciated if, like the work of a bad painter all the more sought after because his "style" is easily recognizable, he arms himself with some easily identifiable characteristics that will link him to an easily identifiable flock: bridge player, mountaineer, or golfer—it matters little which. By the sport that he plays or the car that he drives, by the club he belongs to, or the religion that he subscribes to, he may acquire shreds of identity, small, fragile pieces of driftwood caught up in the general flux, to which those shipwrecked in the modern world cling to give themselves the illusion of immovability. Here too, Japan shows the way: snobbishness—if one can still talk of snobbery when the snobs have no other model to ape but themselves—is stronger there than elsewhere, to the joy of German automobile manufacturers and French manufacturers of luxury products. And in this "empire of signs," money becomes the ultimate sign, the common denominator that allows signs to be linked together, to avoid an irremediable fragmentation. This is the magic fluid that carries the flotsam of our lost identities. This pursuit of signs has no end, for it never intersects with meaning, and the billboard men of the modern world can never be assured of carrying the right symbol, as long as the social grammar is in constant flux. How sweet they are, then, those fugitive moments in which modern man may rest his weariness in some professional encounter in which his work is temporarily recognized!

However, in this world in which one must belong to a group before one belongs to oneself, where efficiency requires uniformity, difference has its price; the breaking down of the world into modular elements now permits the creation of a mass-produced difference: it is the combination of elements that creates the unique—a unique combination of standard elements. This industrial manner of creating rarity is reproduced in advances in biology, industry, and marketing. The more our knowledge of cells advances, the better we comprehend that each human being is unique, right down to the biological detail of his organism. And the more the industrial production line is improved, the more it is standardized, so that the same part can be found in different models of car or airplane. But the flexibility of manufacture that makes computerized production lines possible is such that a production line can turn out products that are very different. The combination of options offered ever increases the number of types available, even as standardization is accentuated. And this increasingly precise adjustment of the industrial process is in itself only the reflection of advances achieved in marketing: market research has become more sophisticated, so that instead of proposing an all-purpose product for a heterogeneous assembly of potential clients, it has become possible to multiply both products and commercial "targets," without any further input from the world of craftsmanship. Whether their interest is in an automobile or a package holiday, consumers can henceforth have the impression that they are buying a product that has been specially conceived for them, or at least for the rare combination of diverse characteristics that define the "handpicked" group to which they are flattered to belong.

We are a long way from craftsmanship, but its myths are being appropriated. To break the infinite reflection of mirrors of the world of repetition and uniformity, signatures are needed. From the butcher to the designer, via the maker of fine luggage, the same ambition is manifest: to be able to affix one's stamp on it, in order to sell not simply a suitcase, a sweater, or a ham, but the invention of a "creator." To market the unique, and to sell *la différence*, and at the same time to be able to command the enhanced price that the intrinsic qualities of the product do not in themselves permit, taking the competition into account: increasingly, profits are made on the notional, and a firm's most important asset is not necessarily an industrial process, but its name, insofar as it has been able to promote it. Never has there been more talk of creativity than in this epoch of manufacturers.

In this imperial age, in which no pole has any value in itself, in which people exist only through the connections they are capable of creating, the networks they can develop, and the groupings in which they participate, each pole must attempt to create the illusion that it is unique, that is to say, irreplaceable. In other words, that it stands alone, and not only through its relationship with others.

Designers thus enjoy a particular reverence, the homage rendered to a social logic that is fast disappearing. And it is true that the prestige of a successful star in the entertainment world is priceless, insofar as it cannot be reduced to a simple combination of modular, reproducible elements. Stardom—even mediocre stardom—expresses an irreducible difference that enriches the networked world with a supplementary pole, a pole that (and this is an exception) existed before the relationships it develops. All that is not reproducible thus commands, in the world of repetition, unheard-of prices. In a world that no longer enriches itself except by fragmentation, by an infinite division of the modules of the social Lego, the artist and the work of art are the last open frontier, the ultimate possibility for expansion. Thus, side by side, we have the reality of the multiple and the banal and the religion of the unique—in harmonious coexistence.

But how does this reality of the multiple take shape? How is homogeneity constructed? In the business world, they talk about the "corporate mission," and in public life, of national identity. The less hierarchical a society is, and the more power is diffused, the more necessary it is that such a national identity, such a corporate mission, be imposed. For the play of microdecisions to function effectively, each anonymous actor must be on the same footing as the other actors, must feel himself carried up in the same flux, as if he truly belongs in the same milieu—in the sense that one talks of an "aquatic medium." Does this call into question the age of networked power? If a corporate director or politician must call the tune, and transmit the message, does not this strategic choice emanating from the top reestablish an institutional pole, a center, a principle of organization from which everything else radiates? If an exterior element slips into the infinite repetition of mirrors, is the whole construction not called into question?

It is here that we must return to our meteorological analogy and admit that great effects can be produced by small causes. Certainly, the boss makes choices and decides between different options—in short, defines a strategy. And it would be false to claim that the analysis of the available data imposes a choice upon him, that there is only one good policy, or one good strategy. But it is increasingly rare that any given choice has decisive consequences: decisions are fragmented and choices cancel each other out. The risk is greater that there be no decision than that there be a wrong decision. The imperial world has a horror of ruptures, and change operates within it by small increments.

Each choice resonates with previous choices: and the corporate mission or the national identity results as much from the memory of previous decisions as from more recent choices. There are in fact collective legacies, an accretion of beliefs and habits that for the most part we would be wrong to try to jettison. It will thus be noted that certain decisions, because they resonate with some great stereotypes fashioned by history, have what one might call more echo. Are they the better for it?

The example of France, a nation that, more than others, has lived off a delicate construct of memory, is eloquent in this regard. It was General de Gaulle's talent to inscribe his action in the tradition of a history full of glorious stereotypes, from Joan of Arc to the heroes of the Resistance. Thanks to him, the French were able to lie to themselves and impress the world. They convinced themselves that they resisted Germany in 1940 and that they won their independence from the United States when they left the integrated command of NATO in 1966. Such comforting beliefs helped them to live, gave them back confidence in themselves, and no doubt the France of the 1960s would have had less resilience if it had not been able, thanks to Gaullism, to paper over the break of 1940 and to reestablish the continuity of a history that it would have be glorious. But was this any more than a clever illusion? And was Gaullist voluntarism not also an intelligent and temporary use of a few stereotypes at a given moment? The revolt of May 1968 showed, for the first time, the limits of that endeavor. To use the jargon of communications consultants, one must never separate internal communication and external communication. One of General de Gaulle's mistakes was to ignore this: the dislocation between the exterior image and the interior image was one of the causes of the May explosion. And twenty-five years later, on another front, our difficulty in seeing France as it really was in 1940 prevents us from seeing Germany as it really is in 1993. The mediocrity of France in 1940 prevents us from seeing the banality of Germany in 1993, and we have trouble overcoming an inferiority complex that distorts the relationship between the two countries. The resonance that helped France to progress in the 1960s is a hindrance in the early 1990s. We must switch conformisms today, but the French do not know how to.

The corporate mission and the identity of a nation are the givens, far more than they are the effects of a voluntary construct. They can only be modified progressively, by maneuvers on the periphery. The strength of the idea of the nation, in its European definition, was precisely that of being the fruit of history, of being a memory, without claiming to become a truth.

Therein lies the danger of the present period: if the elements of memory fail us, if the "given" of the social entity is stripped away, the conformity that is so necessary to the smooth functioning of our societies, rather than being a habit as unconstricting as an old garment made supple by years of wear, can become a constant effort, and can stiffen into a totalitarian reflex. If the space occupied by the nation is no longer defined by memory, if the space for democracy answers only to a functional definition (a space in which decision making is governed by an agreed procedure), the tension between us and them—those who are like us and those who are not like us—is effectively the only means left to us to define a social group threatened with dislocation by the multiplication of the levels of sovereignty. If we have lost the memory of our national history, if the management of our affairs is parceled out on several levels—the township, the region, the nation, the continent, the world—how will we be able to establish relationships with others, relationships that we nevertheless know are the basis of our power?

7

RELIGIONS WITHOUT GOD

Extreme primitivism joins extreme modernism. As if the hymn of
Japanese enterprise had to replace the chants of the cathedrals,
"televangelism" has succeeded the preaching of the saints, and
the sect takes in those no longer attracted to the convent. All these
are signs that there is not that incompatibility between religion—or religiosity—and modernity that the scientists of the
nineteenth century thought they discerned. The most interesting
phenomenon, however, is not the so-called return of the religious,
which presupposes that religious aspiration at some point disappeared from our hearts, but the multitude of new forms that this
aspiration can assume. Contrary to Montesquieu's predictions
two and a half centuries ago, the historical dynamic started by the
Age of Enlightenment does not lead to the death of religions, but
to their revival in new, and sometimes degraded, forms.

The Roman republic died at that point in time that also saw the
religious fermentation that gave rise to Christianity. We live in an
era that is in certain respects comparable. The political sphere, after freeing itself from its religious origins, is dying today from its
own liberation. It is disappearing with a great clangor, and we are

often left only with rituals, in a world deserted by politics just as it was deserted by the gods—magical loyalties that we cling to to bring a sense of the imperative into our hazardous lives.

In fact, the progress of the scientific age does not distance us from religion, but brings us closer to it. Accustomed to procedures and computer commands, we live in a world of rituals, and machines represent in the world of things what priests do in the world of gods; moreover, a machine may serve as seer, producing a horoscope far more detailed than the best of fortune-tellers. In the abstraction of the imperial world, religion suddenly seems more real. We have the same avid relationship with religion as children have with Batman and Ghostbusters: science fiction is the heir to novels of chivalry, a technological staging of the past, when our brother humans were endowed with passions. Heroes whose metallic carapace could represent either the armor of knights of the Middle Ages or the robots of the electronic age engage in interplanetary combat with magic swords.

No surprise, then, if, two thousand years after the beginnings of the Christian era, and just as science considers itself all-powerful, religions are developing through their most magical features; no surprise that ritual prevails over metaphysics. What we seek in religions is precisely their contingency: in a world in which everything has a function but nothing has a sense, we revere indeterminacy as the last refuge of meaning. The religions of the imperial age are thus at the opposite pole from the "natural religion" of the Enlightenment philosophers. They are all the more successful in that they avoid the deductions of reason; they do not seek to make themselves "believable," and deist compromises appear to them to be a bad bargain. This is a trait common to the sects and the new fundamentalisms: that they do not try to keep themselves up-to-date. They neither claim to be "modern" nor universal, and this refusal, far from diminishing their allure, increases it.

In the poor countries in which the nation-state has not taken root, religions aspire to infuse new life into politics and give it meaning again. Both Islamic and Hindu fundamentalism breathe their conquering energy into societies that the ill-digested shock of economic modernity has profoundly disoriented. And the contrast between our disabused lassitude and the revolutionary determination of the Islamists frightens us, as though, after the death of Communism, Islam could offer a new global political project: a project all the more dangerous in that we have supposedly lost faith in our own democratic universalism. Politics may be dead in the most affluent societies, but it revives, virulently, carried by religion, to make itself at home in poorer societies left at the wayside by the integration of the networked age.

However, in the less than twelve years since its foundation, the first Islamic republic has aged almost as much as the Communist movement did in seventy years. The Iranian revolution tried to repaint in the colors of Islam a political project that owed much to the Marxist ideologies that gripped the Third World during the cold war era. But the bureaucratic management of the Islamic foundations has been no more effective than Soviet planning.

Islam as a political force has shown itself to be incapable of proposing, as Communism tried to do after 1917, a global response to the tensions that had fostered its appearance. That is its opportunity and its limitation. It will not destroy, as Communism has destroyed the empire of the czars, the societies in which it implants itself. It has in fact quickly given up regulating every aspect of life in society, and it coexists without real difficulties with an entirely capitalist economic logic, even though its prohibition of usury entails some camouflage action.

This failure of the political ambitions of Islamism brings Islam back to its real religious dimension. Its aim is to change not institutions but the consciousness of men. The renewal of Islam is fueled by the myriad frustrations engendered by the poverty and the rootlessness of large cities, but the response that it offers is not political in nature. The neofundamentalisms that have succeeded Islamism do not propose a new world order but, more modestly, the proximity of a community, mimicking, at the level of personal relationships, the just society that, on the political level, has been abandoned as a project. This profound pessimism explains how neofundamentalist militants are at once little interested in proselytization and extremely intolerant. Their principal ambition is not to expand the community of believers but to constitute a homogeneous community, one that is all the more comfortable and reassuring in that it is turned in on itself. In this sense, Islamic militancy reproduces certain features of the West's sects. It arrives at communion only by orchestrating a separation.

At the same time, this wish to affirm values, this contestation of the social order and of established religious hierarchies recalls Luther. There is, in the refusal of the compromises of politics, a powerful appeal to individual conscience: the just society will not be made from above, by the advent of a good prince, but from below, conscience by conscience. That ambition, which is built on the failure of politics and on the marriage of politics and religion, will perhaps have as profound an impact on Islam as did the Protestant Reformation on Christianity: its effect on history has not yet ceased to be felt.

In fact, it corresponds to a profound need of the imperial age, whether it is a question of societies dislocated by the dynamic of the networks and of the global economy, or of the constricted world of the most advanced economies. In both cases, the prominence of the traditional group has disappeared, leaving only helpless individuals, free of affiliation or whose only affiliation is functional, through a trade or skill—a curious contrast between our behavior, increasingly locked into constraints that we have no control over, and our thoughts, all the more free in that they are without consequences. In a world in which everything has a function but in which nothing has any meaning, "religion" is henceforth the only constraint freely accepted, or even desired.

In the wealthy countries, this "religious" aspiration is expressed in a different way but betrays the same disappointment with politics. In this respect, the development of humanitarian organizations will serve as a good example. Having given up on finding solutions to human misfortunes in a political order, the new militants of the humanitarian have made emergency their principle of action. They certainly hoped that politics would pick up the baton, but, increasingly, humanitarian action takes the place of the political, to the point where it has become the only realm of action outside a given state that can count on public support—a strange situation, in which politics can find acceptance only by giving up on political ambition.

To save a human life, to deal with the immediate, to set aside overgeneral principles in order to confront a particular situation—this characteristic pragmatism of humanitarian action corresponds to the exigencies of an individual morality, in which a life saved is justification in itself. Political entities, managing the collective destiny, no longer in effect intervene between the abstract community of men and the multitude of individual destinies. Humanitarian militancy gives expression to this disappointment with political institutions, and is concerned to recreate concrete solidarities in a world that has become too abstract. These militants rediscover, in engagement and the dangers of action, a feeling of belonging to a human community—and not only as a result of the constraints of the functional world. Humanitarian action is a means of escaping the intolerable encounter between the solitary individual and a globality that cannot be mastered, but which it is no longer possible to ignore.

In a world of limited resources, we guess that our extraordinary wealth cannot be made universal. The search for the universal, far from giving meaning to our particular destinies, thus frightens us. It reveals our contradictions and our renunciations. Humanitarian action thus offers to the wealthy the same sensation of a moral experience, individual but shared, that Islam offers to the poor. No one seeks any longer, in the abstract, to cure the miseries of the world. Poverty has found a face again, and an immediate solidarity, born of urgency and suffering, sets in. Having lost the illusion of a political solution that would put an end to misfortune and would make a community from the multitude of human destinies, we devote ourselves to others, rather than to the human race.

This concrete experience of a communication with others—with a few other people—is what we demand from religion today. When everything is directed toward the universal, it affirms difference, a difference that is no longer political but moral. When frontiers fall, it forms the basis for the specificity of groups; it raises new barriers where, yesterday, it made the ramparts fall. The metaphysical problem of our age is not in fact to reveal the universal in the inequality of social conditions, but to found differentiation in the limitless standardization of the networks. In the postnational age, we do not aspire to a henceforth undefined solidarity, but to limit the scope of solidarity while rediscovering it in our everyday lives.

Religion in the imperial age thus inherits the functions that the nation filled in the institutional age. It divides rather than unites. And if it organizes social communion, it is often—as is the case with the sects—by way of separation, and not on a universal scale. In a world of uniformity and homogenization, religion allows us to escape universal abstraction, and to rediscover, in the archipelago of modern solitudes, the sense of our particularity.

In the past, the shepherd, lost in his nocturnal solitude, searched in the multitude of twinkling stars for the trace of a unifying principle that could link him again to the community of men; and the success of the great monotheistic religions certainly owes much to this need to escape the isolation—at once geographical and social—that has for so long characterized the human condition. Our problem is quite different. We are just as lonely, but our solitude is that of the man lost in the crowd, mobile and without attachments. Our anguish is not to be separated from the great whole, but to lose ourselves in it. The heavens are empty, and we are assailed by a multitude of signs, signs that do not refer to any unifying totality.

Of all the countries that have reached into economic modernity, Japan is perhaps the one that has found the most efficient answer to this dilemma. In contrast with the Islamic intellectual who cobbles together the illusion of a transcendent totality in which, in the syncretism of the self-taught, citations from the Koran are jumbled with borrowings from contemporary science, and in contrast with the European militant whose humanitarian engagement remains an act of faith in the unity of the human condition, many Japanese in effect accept the fragmentation of the world as a natural given of our condition. It is in this sense that the Japanese approach to religion is, in its archaism, profoundly modern. In rejecting transcendence and the search for principles, but in divining the infinite multitude of signs, this approach sacralizes a plural world that no longer has a metaphysical unity; it transforms an atheism that most men have not the strength of heart to support into an imperial pantheism that is far more livable. The group, incarnate in the emperor, is in itself its own divinity. The emperor is the man-god who has attained the absolute void and thus offers a life-model, entirely defined by the regard of others and by his own presence to others. Shut in his palace, surrounded by sweeping roofs, remaining for long periods with only formal communications with the world, separated from his subjects by an oppressive ritualism, the emperor of Japan embodies, as it were, the central vacuum.

In a multiple world, no longer governed by any political or philosophical order, we cannot ourselves claim any interior unity. Wracked by sensations, subject to multiple impulses, our lives file past like a shadow play. There is nothing left but to adore a blade of grass, a moonbeam, a transitory emotion—poor meager treasures of our fragmented world. The Copernican revolution robbed planet Earth of its central place, but at least, with the sun, preserved the idea of a center. It is that idea that is in the process of dying. The triumph of the relative, this victory of relation over principle, does not distance us from religion, but changes the nature of the religious vigil. Polytheism no doubt has more of a future than monotheism.

By religion, one must in fact now understand not the belief in a transcendence, a God, of principles, but, far more modestly, that sum of rites and what might be called habits, "habits of the heart" that—as Tocqueville said of America—shape our behavior.

There is thus no incompatibility between the abstract globalization of the imperial age and the archaism of religious fragmentation. The second is the natural consequence of the first, and the two phenomena are not contradictory; they do not contest the same terrain, and the future could well result in their triumphant coexistence. As under the Roman empire, and up to a certain point for the same reasons, we will perhaps see both the state of law and a religious effervescence:

A state of law deprived of all philosophical reference to natural law, reduced to an ensemble of rules with no other basis than the daily administered proof of its smooth functioning; a law that is neither the expression of sovereignty, of a political entity—in Islamic countries, the disdain for political institutions and the insistence on Islamic law, the sharia, is, in a way, the first example of a "law without a state"—nor the translation in society of a natural order deciphered by human reason. This law would be an elegant and practical way of managing process, as useful as a computer program. One does not prostrate oneself before a computer program.

Religions that cater to difference and thus identity, the possibility of believing without this belief being the by-product of the pitiless logic of the networks; a polytheism that has chosen the diversity of things and of men, but which is incapable of the universal.

Through this religious engagement, we participate in a humanity that no longer knows how to manifest itself in the empty arena of politics, and we recover the feeling of belonging that we have lost with the disappearance of the body politic.

The proliferation of the law in the imperial age and the proliferation of religions thus complement each other a great deal. Confronted with the multiplication of necessities without principles, we are pleased to adore a few principles without necessity, but in total independence: the latter are not predicated on the former. The third Rome, that of Moscow and Communism, claimed to link the two, and to have founded a terrestrial religion by conferring a meaning on social and historical necessities.

The empire that is emerging has no such pretensions. The law that it institutes has no state, no God, no foundation. It places no God in the sky nor makes one descend to earth. It is, strictly speaking, atheistic: it leaves the field free for new religions.

8

THE GOLDEN CALF

If it took only procedures to unify an imperial world fragmented by religions and communities, the empire would not exist. But modern power is not only abstract, it expresses itself in money, the universal passageway between all forms of power—the great unifier, unreal and trivial, of the imperial age and its motley of religions. It is on this account that corruption deserves to be analyzed, not as a secondary phenomenon but as the emblem of our time, and perhaps, as the only "religion" that has a universal vocation today.

We like to think that corruption is an archaic phenomenon, a regrettable relic of a time in which no distinction was made between private fortune and public wealth. The fact that in certain Third World countries bribes must be handed out to the authorities is shocking to us, but does not make us uneasy on our own account: we interpret it as a delay in the construction of the nation-state, not as a threat. That corruption should manifest itself in Japan, a country on the cutting edge of economic development, is more troubling: we reassure ourselves by attributing it to something peculiar to the Japanese. If corruption crops up in the old countries of Europe, in Germany or France, or in the United States, the only response remaining to us is to insist that it is an anomaly.

At no point do we ask ourselves whether corruption, far from being an abnormal, pathological phenomenon, is not one of the characteristic features of a developed industrial society.

In earlier chapters it has been shown to what point the modern form of power is found in the diffusion of information, and not in its retention. Power is not to limit the knowledge of others—we will be needing them—but to be capable of mobilizing the knowledge of others. The consequence of this new situation is an extraordinary multiplication of information, which banalizes the savants, and valorizes the network. Social relations, like power relations, have been profoundly changed by it. Instead of the traditional pyramid, in which the "specialists" at the bottom operated under bosses a little less specialized, right up to the "generalist in chief," the structure of power no longer reflects any more than a certain mode of routing decisions within the organizational labyrinth. There is thus no longer a point at which the decision is taken, but a series of steps in the course of which a decision is progressively shaped. It is on this terrain that a new form of corruption can flourish.

The traditional mode, which is spreading in some countries of the Third World, corresponds to a "pre-statist" society: big bosses make big decisions—and big bribes can influence these decisions. Those who make decisions are identified, and corruption develops not because it is impossible to control it—the circuits of decision are clear—but because of a political refusal to assume control: there is no state. This is not the situation in the industrialized countries, where the will to fight corruption exists but where the structures of decision make this control more difficult every day.

Because those taking part in the making of a decision are multiple, the potential targets of the corrupters are numerous, too. Certainly, each of the actors can make only—if it's possible to say this—a little bit of the decision: and this gives, at the margins, an inflection, a twist, to a process that outstrips the "bit of the decision" itself. Can this same twist perhaps qualify as the decision? Reacting to a multitude of information, to a superabundance of data, attempting to take into account the contradictory interests of different pressure groups, the modern bureaucrat sees himself less and less as an intercessor charged with asserting an elusive public interest and more and more as a sort of social engineer, facilitator of a "game" that is a law unto itself.

In such a universe, an excess of information cancels itself out, and the fragmented process of making the decision reduces the margin of choices: as already shown, it is almost never a case of choosing between two radically opposed outcomes but rather of taking the responsibility for shelving a solution that one will never be sure was inferior to the one chosen. The same evolution can be observed in choosing between individuals, whether in the case of hirings or of business relationships. Certainly, the era of the privileges of the ancient nobility and of honorary appointments is gone. But in another way, "classic" preference reemerges: a glut of diplomas cancels out diplomas, and in a society built on networks, competition eliminates the mediocre and allows only the best to survive. How should they be chosen? Whether it is a matter of decisions, corporations, or of individuals, the problem is the same.

The age of information, by overwhelming us with knowledge,

makes illusory the hope of making a choice on a purely technical basis. On each occasion, several choices, several candidates may be equally qualified. The "classic" response is thus the most logical response. To choose what one knows, to reintroduce loyalties in this abstract world, are so many means of reassurance and of filling the vacuum left by the disappearance of the political. When the quality of the information is assured, the quality of the contact becomes essential, and the decisions, as in the case of choosing personnel, are made at the margins, on that selfsame quality. Given a choice between two enterprises of equal repute, between two individuals of comparable credentials, the one that is the most "familiar" will be chosen.

In a different world, in which the public servant is the repository of a body of knowledge and the representative of the public interest, the separation is clear between an attitude of integrity, which demands isolation, and corruption, which begins with contact. In a world in which power flows from a capacity to make connections rather than from knowledge, in which the public interest and the private try to link up for the sake of efficiency, corruption becomes a dirty word, which fails to describe the imperceptible trajectory through which one passes from contact to dependency, from information to influence.

In a society that would like to believe it can make utilitarianism its operating principle and the foundation of its social contract, corruption is only harmful if it is not generalized, for then it translates into an unequal access to the "services" of public authority. But as soon as this public authority restricts itself to providing "services," it is not unusual, in a market economy, for these services to be remunerated. Certainly, one can regret that certain officials appropriate for themselves a remuneration that should have been shared among the collaborators who contributed to providing the service. This critique targets a mode of organization more than a principle: From the moment that the administration has become sufficiently diversified and specialized—when it no longer appears as the expression of a collective and distinct will of the multitude of private interests, but as a simple provider of services—the "commitment" of officials to the results could be presented as a form of modernization of the pay for public office, except that it would be left to show that the decision that procures a remuneration for the person who makes it is a necessarily less good decision than one that does not entail such a remuneration (for that would be to affirm that the demand that can be paid for is necessarily less legitimate than that which is not).

When power lies in communication, the law can certainly interdict the remuneration of communication, but taking it off the market—as justified as that may be for the smooth operation of political institutions, which presuppose a clear separation between public interests and private interests—is so contrary to the spirit of the system that it can only generally postpone the moment of "corruption." The official who commands a good network will, for a hefty sum, make this network available to the private company that eventually will recruit him. Will he then feel that he is giving in to corruption? Not necessarily, because he is thereby contributing, like his Japanese colleagues who practice what they call *amakudari*, to the setting of the social mayonnaise.

Remunerating the highest functionaries on credit, through the prospect of a cozy sinecure later, and politicians with ready cash—by gratuities that finance not just electoral campaigns—

this compromise that the Japanese are today criticizing may perhaps have a future outside Japan. To the administration, it handily saves face in protecting appearances; to politicians, perhaps fearing that they will be deprived of the reality of power, it offers an agreeable consolation. On the whole, is this arrangement worse than the illusion of political control over the administration, an illusion that demoralizes the functionaries without truly reestablishing democracy? A depressing alternative.

In fact, our instinctive rejection of corruption is all that remains of another world, fast disappearing, in which the independence of the political sphere was a given. But there is some naïveté in wanting politicians to retain their high calling, priests of a vanished religion. How could there still be a clergy, if there is no flock? So one should not be surprised if even in France, where the idea of "public service" has survived longer than in other industrialized countries (and through this idea the affirmation of a public interest that cannot be reduced to the sphere of private interests), high political office is losing its appeal. No government any longer dares to grant its officials a salary commensurate with that of equivalent functions in the private sector, and this attitude meets with the approval of a public convinced that the services rendered are not of equal value. As for moral remuneration, in social prestige, that has long since disappeared. Officials, conscious that the administration functions but poorly, lost their respect for themselves at the same time that they were losing that of the people they have jurisdiction over. Yielding to corruption can be for the most cynical only an agreeable way of convincing oneself that one still has some value.

Minimizing the upheaval that we are witnessing, some claim that the decline of public office, such as that to be seen in France, implies only an adjustment of the relationship between the public sphere and the private sphere. The hypocritical "French model" of an apolitical administration, ensuring the permanence of the public interest, is replaced by the "American model," or a more political administration, whose higher echelon changes with each change in majority. And soon, instead of a national elite that begins its career in the administration and ends it in the private sector, we shall see the opposite formula appear, under which the managers of the private sector come, their fortunes made, to bring their experience of business to the management of public interests. This appeasing interpretation makes a mockery of the prospects of the lower rungs of the administration, as it does of the decision-making process itself. Private enterprises have learned that one does not mobilize a group of people by parachuting in over their heads managers who have not shared their lives. And they know that good decisions are shared decisions, arrived at over a long process—a point that eludes the American schema. In fact, the politicians who think they can today replace the functionaries of yesterday take orders from a demoralized government bureaucracy, and this direction is itself an illusion: faithful in this to the "American model," they manage perceptions and symbols—the only domain in which there remains real freedom to maneuver—more than they make decisions in the traditional sense of the word. In filling a ministerial post, the recourse to such and such a leading light of the business world thus fairly often has the result, not so much of transferring to the public sphere the supposed efficiency of private enterprise, as in conferring on the state, in the eyes of the outside world but not in those of its servitors, a prestige that it no longer has the means to obtain by itself.

By their contribution to a public authority that has lost its self-esteem, businessmen do not make a corporation out of the state, but validate the idea that the state is respectable only if it resembles an enterprise. How could this be the case as long as the very possibility of such appointments and the rift they open up between a supposed echelon of decision and a supposed echelon of execution is completely contrary to the operating principles of a modern enterprise?

The institutionalization of separate poles of power was a wholly political notion, corresponding to an age in which the public interest was presented as being in opposition to the private interest. Efficiency today demands exactly the opposite: an integrated society in which the intensity of relations allows for the optimal circulation of information. Corruption is now only an archaic word through which those nostalgic for another age bitterly describe the inevitable value accorded to networked power.

The deal is hallowed as the only truth of our age, and any demand that is solvent is a legitimate demand. How can we not make the golden calf the supreme divinity?

Having lost the authority conferred on them by their role as depositories of a public interest, overtaken by the globalization of the circuits of wealth, in competition with the wealth of new actors, manipulated by interests often more powerful than themselves, the nation-states, exhausted and sickly, will increasingly be suspected of condemning corruption only to protect what power is left to them.

The proliferation of financial "scandals" in the great democracies is thus not an anomaly, but the logical consequence of the triumph of the only universality that remains to us, that of money, the measure of the success both of individuals and of societies, a common token that permits the establishment of an immediate communication with our "equals,"—equals in the reverence that they share for the golden calf, finally offered to the government, if not for the appropriation of all.

9

IMPERIAL VIOLENCE

Will the abstract universality of the imperial world be robust enough to resist the very concrete force of specific experiences? If the nation-states are no more, will wars of religion replace the wars between nations, and will the logic of Lebanization be stronger than the imperial logic? Or are we headed toward a world without violence, pacified by the death of ideas and the triumph of the golden calf? To answer such questions, it will not do to look toward Iran, even if the flagging of the Islamic revolution there demonstrates, a fortiori, the difficulties religion has in acquiring a political dimension in our imperial age.

It is to the very heart of the world of the networks, the most prosperous parts of the planet, that we must turn our attention. It is not insignificant that, in the process of general homogenization, Japan is able to remain so "exotic." Will these "religions" that we have inherited prevent us from converging on a new "catholicity"—one that will embrace with similar uniformity the spaces that have been deserted by politics?

It is too early to say whether an essential, irreducible difference will impose itself between the three poles of the triad, and particularly between Asia and the two other poles—a difference capable of resisting the layering of the diffusion of power. Will we in turn become "Asiatic," as the logic of the imperial age is impelling us to become? Or will we be inclined to resist? Will the European model, whose ideal we have imposed upon the whole world, in the form of twins, the nation-state and democracy, disappear without a jolt? Will we accept an apolitical mode of organization, well suited to the constraints of this new world but profoundly alien to the memory of what we have been? All our culture is opposed to such a homogenization, and it is thus highly possible that the worldwide phenomenon of the diffusion of power may not have the same effects in Europe, North America, and Asia. It may also be that instead of a single empire, several are forming. In the world of the networks and of the diffusion of power, their frontiers would necessarily be uncertain, for political affiliation would be only a secondary characteristic. For an example, one need think only of the Russian territories of the Far East, so close to Japan and China, which could become the object of power struggles. If that were to happen, the process that should prevent conflicts would instead risk rendering them insoluble: each sphere, obeying its own dynamic, its "religion," would be caught up in a movement all the more difficult to halt because it would no longer have a "center" on which to act. That was the experience of Japan in the interwar period, carried away not by the will of one man, like the Germany of Hitler, but by the incapacity of a society that had no center to resist the forces that it had been subjected to. The experience that was Japan's in particular is today, in the imperial age, the shared destiny of all men, carried away as they are by processes that they cannot control.

One can see how this incomplete homogenization of the world

could cast us into an impasse: three poles become at once uncontrollable and impossible to coordinate. The mediocre functioning of the Group of Seven industrialized countries during the last several years shows clearly, in the economic domain, the impasses to which a world that is at once unified and deprived of a center can lead. Could this confrontation lead one day to structured, organized violence, on the model of the wars of the national age but with the means of the nuclear age?

This, happily, remains fairly unlikely, insofar as nuclear confrontation in the past forty years is the abstract apotheosis of violence in the national age. From the mass recruitments of the armies of the French Revolution to the nuclear hostage-taking of entire peoples, through the mass deaths of two world wars, the complete cycle of a concentration of violence—a violence inscribed within the logic of the concentration of power in the age of the nations—has run its course.

By making war the ultimate expression of the will of whole populations, and not only the sport of princes, the national age had invented the idea of total war: henceforth, the nations, as good subjects of the institutional age, had to act out to the end their logic of power, in "mutual assured destruction" that made the idea of a limited war an anomaly. People killed with far more gusto in the name of the nation than they had in the name of the king. The collective will to live, with its corollary, the will to kill, was, moreover, a sentiment stronger than the sense of duty and honor of the soldiers of the ancien régime. The nation could organize to its profit, in a pyramidal construction of power, all the latent energies dispersed on its territory. The immense armies of conscription that faced each other in two world wars created, in the bloody melee of battles, a kind of collective subject that expressed the nation. And since this collective no longer had only to defeat armies, but to destroy the very bases of the power of a nation, the distinction between the vanguard and the rear, between the military and the civilians, gradually lost its meaning. The terror bombings, the mobilization by propaganda of entire peoples, whose spirit of aggression had to be whipped up, completed the process that had begun a century and a half earlier at the battle of Valmy. The sword had definitively ceased to be a privilege, and death had made itself democratic.

Nuclear deterrence is the culmination of this evolution, in which the effects of power are distributed insofar as power is concentrated. On the one hand, there is no longer any place, in nuclear war, for individual destinies, and the promise of a mass death has replaced mass conscription. On the other hand, through political and technical necessity, nuclear deterrence concentrates in one individual a power that puts the lives of everyone at risk. A strange end for violence in the institutional age. The selfsame logic that makes the confrontation between individual wills the foundation of democratic organization propels the nations toward a mutual assured destruction that destroys the very bases of the social contract. For in delegating to a chief of state the responsibility of assuming—for the whole nation—the supreme risk, we are far from the volunteers of the French Revolutionary army at Valmy, and our equality in the face of deterrence is closer to the equality of slaves than that of citizens. The relationship that is established between the mass that undertakes to obey and the solitary man who is burdened with the decision is indeed a far cry from a democratic relationship.

And can we still be said to be citizens, when the credibility of deterrence requires that we turn ourselves not only into hostages but also into takers of hostages, abandoning the universality of values that is a premise of the democratic debate, so that we no longer see the civil population of the enemy as the citizens of another nation but only the indivisible and abstract elements of a nation that we must vow to destroy? Slaves submitting to the decisions of a chief to whom we have consigned our lives, we are obliged, in order to ensure the security of our nation, to give up the very principles on which our attachment to democracy was founded. No surprise, then, that the nuclear democracies in this twilight of the institutional age produce citizens who are passive and cynical. Nuclear deterrence, the culmination of the institutional age, given the extreme concentration of power that it implies, is thus also the beginning of the imperial age, by the destruction of the political entity that it organizes. The exaltation of the nation-subject is achieved at the expense of the citizen-subjects of the institutional order.

The growing dislocation between the centralization of the nuclear decision and the process of diffusion of power that is characteristic of the imperial age nevertheless calls into question the very basis of deterrence. This can be clearly seen in two situations that appear contradictory: in the former Soviet Union, where nuclear weapons increase the dangers of the process of breakup; and in the European Community, where the possession by Britain and France of the atomic bomb contributes to the security of Europe but complicates the establishment of a European defense mechanism exercising real power. Nuclear deterrence was conceived for a world of nation-states with clearly defined competences and frontiers. The absolute threat and the risks that it carries with it do not easily accommodate the relative and shared sovereignties of an imperial age that blurs frontiers.

So, just as a tree transplanted into another climate sheds its leaves, nuclear deterrence could one day appear as an intellectual abstraction, detached from the political conditions that prevailed at its birth. Medieval fortresses, monumental testimony of a vanished world, survived the artillery that breached their walls for some time, but did not resist the reinforcement of royal power that destroyed the feudal system. The same thing may happen with nuclear deterrence. For a time, the powers that be in the nuclear states may justify themselves by the very immensity of their responsibility to retain an exceptional power in their own hands. But the moment will come when this concentration of power, so contrary to the logic of diffusion of power, will be seen as intolerable and dangerous; so, instead of deriving the status of the authorities from the possession of nuclear weapons, the desire to adapt this role to the exigences of the imperial age will lead to questions—if not about the possession of weapons as such, at least about the very principles of dissuasion. Perhaps, with the help of the threat of proliferation, we will seek to "tame" such weapons: to use them, rather than threatening to use them. At the same time, the collegiality of the decision threatens to become a constraint. Will nuclear deterrence survive such developments? But the crisis of deterrence does not necessarily herald a return to the classical forms of war.

To those who fear that the disappearance of the nation-states will also entail an end to the democracies, one might point out that this age was one of an extreme and formidable concentration of violence. The era into which we are entering will doubtless never know the concentration of violence of the last two world wars. No nation today is capable of mobilizing such gigantic forces around an idea. The great bloodbaths of the twentieth century were made possible by the conflation of the absolute power of a nation-state and of a "religion"—nationalist, National Socialist, or Communist—that gave it direction. If the directed violence of the age of the nation-states is to resurface within the triad of Europe, America, and Asia, not only would several empires have to emerge, but the ideologies of the future would have to be capable of forging a unique strategic direction in each empire—and this in a world fragmented by the complexity of the networks. Such an enterprise would fortunately be very difficult.

This application of the disciplines of the imperial age to the domain of violence and of war does not mean, however, that it will be an age of peace and tranquillity. We have seen earlier how the logic of the networks shows itself better able to prevent disputes than to resolve them. To dissolve the multitude of small differences in the acid of conformity is a method that has its limitations, and one can see all kinds of tensions today that, not only on the margins of the networked world but at its very heart, will continue to create imbalances, movements, and conflicts.

In what form will the violence that the imperial world will not be able to prevent manifest itself? Is it a relic of the vanishing institutional logic, or is it its role to be—like corruption, conformity, and religiosity—an indispensable attribute of the new age?

The violence of the age of the networks, the violence of the time of the empires, has every chance of being more diffuse, less extreme, but not at all more rare. The traditional distinctions hitherto considered fundamental will become blurred. Internal security and external security will no longer be in opposition. The difference between states (which according to Max Weber's formula supposedly have the "monopoly of legitimate violence") and all the rest will be more problematic. On the one hand, the exercise of violence by a state ensnared in the networks of the imperial world will become illegitimate, not to say impossible, and other structures will be organized—police forces charged with enforcing norms rather than the expression of a sovereignty. On the other hand, the vulnerability of "networked" societies to outside disturbance will be wedded to sophistication of weaponry—armaments both more powerful and easier to use—blurring the distinction between public violence and private violence.

In the economic sphere—as already shown—the weakening of certain states could combine with the rise to power of "private" agents (drug traffickers, for example) to muddy the distinction between the state domain and that of what are called private interests. The same goes for violence, which will become privatized. Armies, too, as has been seen in the former Yugoslavia, will become privatized: the states will divest themselves of their responsibilities, sometimes by tactical skill, sometimes because they are unable to exercise them. The impossibility of categorically attributing a given terrorist act to a particular state, the criminalization of politics, and the politicization of crime will gradually establish a continuity between two activities that previously were separated: war and crime. Finally, the media unification of the world will no doubt encourage the wealthiest to try to help the most disadvantaged. But the first consequence of such efforts, expended on societies in which all political order will have disappeared, will be to raise the level of violence: where everyone is pitted against each other, wealth permits the wolves to be more effective in their cruelty. People will die from a burst of machine-gun fire, instead of dying of malnutrition.

The frightful spasms of war in the twentieth century supposed a world of nation-states with boundaries sufficiently distinct for war to make a clear, historical break. The diffusion of power should make such ruptures more difficult. It is perhaps reassuring to think that there will never again be a 1 August 1914 or a 1 September 1939. World war will not succeed peace. But there will no longer ever be any peace.

The imperial age is an age of a diffuse and continuous violence. There will no longer be any territory or frontier to defend, but only order—operating methods—to protect. And this abstract security is infinitely more difficult to ensure than that of a world in which geography commanded history. Neither rivers nor oceans protect the delicate mechanisms of the imperial age from a menace as multiform as the empire itself.

Because our wealth is linked less and less to the possession of territories, the invader has nothing to invade. But between the spaces in which the logic of the networks rules and those in which it is still secondary, no clear separation can be established, so that it will be more and more difficult to ignore what is happening at our margins. If we were to entertain the illusion of hemming violence up in external ghettoes and of recreating "cordons sanitaires," such an attempt at isolation would be condemned to failure by the globalization of exchanges, the migration of populations, the contagion of pollution, and the eventual diffusion of arms of massive destruction. Such isolation moreover is profoundly contrary to the logic of the imperial world, a world without frontiers and without a one-dimensional identity. The wars of the future will be wars that have no front.

The empire will thus not be an island of order surrounded by "new barbarians." The supposed barbarians will have no more political unity than the empire. The barbarians are within the empire, and the empire secretes its own barbarians. The growing so-phistication of the networks simultaneously multiplies the exclu-sions and the vulnerabilities, the opportunities for rejection and the occasions of impasse. In a system that is no longer governed by a pyramidal and centralized hierarchy, one can certainly hope that no breakdown, no sabotage is decisive; the circuits, the net-works, recompose themselves around the affected zone, in an al-most biological fashion. Nevertheless, the architecture of the net-works, while it multiplies the possibilities for connection, also multiplies the possible points of attack. The constant concern to reduce the likelihood of uncertainty and the unpredictable re-duces the tolerance for breakdowns and errors. No error is irrepa-rable, but every error has consequences. In a world in which there is no proportionality between cause and effect, the demands of security must be geared down. We find it intolerable if an air liner crashes because of a construction defect. Were a few kilo-grams of plutonium to circulate clandestinely—whether stolen from a nuclear installation or made available by a terrorist group—it would become still more intolerable. Modern indus-try's methods of "quality control" will gradually be extended to the entirety of the imperial society: the controls will multiply ac-cording to the occasions for violence and sabotage. The men of the empire, pursuing wars without fronts on all sides, will be nei-ther the soldiers of the king nor the citizens at arms of the repub-lic; they will be policemen, ever alert, ever ready to track down the different, the unknown, the inexplicable.

THE IMPERIAL AGE

9 November 1989: The fall of the Berlin wall—the victory of democracy

Neither Hitler nor Stalin will thus have succeeded in crushing democracy. They wanted to seize power, but they believed in power, and this belief was their downfall. Belief in power circumscribed the struggle, for it defined a political terrain. For an instant, the time of a revolution, the peoples of the East formed a body politic. They experimented with the sovereignty of the people. And now this victory, still so recent, seems threatened, not because the enemy is gathering strength—the threat of that would be more likely to rekindle the initial enthusiasm—but because we no longer know exactly who are the real enemies.

The totalitarian lie was able, through sheer force of terror, to impose its slavery on millions of people. This lie remained identifiable. This will no longer be the case in the societies of the imperial age; there will be no statue of Dzerzhinsky to pull down from its pedestal, only the amorphous mass of a diffuse and imperceptible power. The new order makes policemen of us all, and there is no longer a police chief against whom we may direct our revolt. We are deprived not of liberty, but of the idea of liberty. For two centuries, we have thought of liberty through the spectrum of the political sphere that was needed to organize it. We wanted to be citizens. But citizenship today is only a convenient means of acting out our ill feeling toward the authorities. We have lost the foundation of our dignity as free men, the aspiration of forming a body politic. This indifference has more subtle effects than the tyrannies of antiquity. It is as sweet as a slow and irremediable hemorrhage.

2 August 1990: The invasion of Kuwait—a primitive holdup or an attempt to demarcate the frontiers of the imperial world?

The world of the networks has been able to keep violence at arm's length, with a mixture of cheerful indifference and abstract brutality. Give or take a photo or two, the dead in Iraq were never more than a vague statistic, and the war was a video game. We had no need even to hate. Throughout the conflict, one of the chief concerns of our governments was to control public opinion at home: we were no more ready for sacrifice than we were for hate, and for the first time in the history of war, the military chiefs— having learned the lesson of the Vietnam War—attached as much importance to managing public opinion and its collective perceptions as to conducting battles. This was a war conducted like a mop-up operation to maintain order: by professionals, whose immense technological superiority permitted them to keep losses to a minimum. The mutineers were crushed and punished. Will this always be the case? A race is on between the spread of technology, which increases the means of violence, and the diffusion of power through the networks, which can bring it to a halt. It may happen that the first outstrips the second. How long will we be able to keep the technical edge that enables us to keep at a distance all that threatens our complex societies? And if violence catches up with us, will we be able to dilute the passion of others in our world without passions? Will complexity prevail over simple ideas, or, on the contrary, will it be carried away by them?

Weaned of collective passions and encircled by hatreds, our human desert could well flare up like a parched savannah. The Roman empire arrogantly ignored the barbarian lands that surrounded it, and this ignorance helped it to live. That alternative is not open to us. What exclusive and brutal "religion" will we invent to justify our happiness in our own eyes, in the midst of so much misery? The natural target of resentment and the envy of billions of other people, will we be able to react in any way other than out of fear, and will we be able to live without passions in a world full of passions? Will the imperial world, in its turn, become prey to fanaticisms it could not conceive of if left to its own logic? And would this diffuse fanaticism be more formidable than the organized, centralized violence of the totalitarianisms of the age of the nations?

There is no answer so far to these questions. We can only sense that the social organization, like a monster that escapes from its creator, is endowed with an unprecedented power, but this power has no goal, so that it is as problematic to determine where it is headed as to claim to hold it in check once it has been released.

We are living in the prehistory of this new age, and the logic of the nation-states will coexist for a long time with the logic of the imperial world. Will this world, like the empires that have gone before it, seek to extend its power in order to reduce the threats that surround it, or will it be paralyzed by the logic that governs it? Those who, on the margins of the empire, would be tempted to defy it are condemned to remain in uncertainty: they could just as well wager on the inability of the postnational power efficiently to resist the classic threat of a nation-state, as to fear the unleashing of imperial power when it is provoked. Saddam Hussein's strategic error was his failure to perceive that the imperial world that was emerging was still organized by nation-states capable of political will. A coalition of states confronted another state. What will happen if the diffusion of power in the imperial world becomes too extensive to permit the mobilization of political will?

2 March 1992: A day like any other in Hong Kong

Men on the run, never separated from their cellular phones. The epitome of the "networked" world. Freedoms and no democracy. A formidable energy that carries the interchangeable units of the human Lego toward ever more contacts and connections. The malls have replaced the cathedrals, and consumption is put on display, magnificently, with an excess of white marble. People ask not "Who are you?" but "Who are you talking to?" From a surfeit of meeting others, one no longer encounters oneself. The solitude of the man who has never known himself. But a productive solitude. All encounters are mediated, standardized by signs: the dollar signs of cash, the trademarks of luxury products. Networkers, people without principles, we are left with nothing but modes of operation. The networked age functions, better than any human organization has ever functioned, but no one knows to what end. The machine has been set in motion. The imperial world is not an ideology, but a process. It secretes conformism—but a conformism that does not know what it should conform to. Is this process self-sustaining, or does it need a frontier, another world, that does not obey the same laws, to maintain its dynamism?

This marvelous and futile movement never ceases to astound us, but sometimes, all of a sudden, a sacrilegious thought occurs: When will we be liberated from the tyranny of progress? Is there no end to the proliferation of the connections of the networks? Where does this anxious compulsion not to leave anything "blank" on the map of the empire come from? The imperial logic is driving toward an indefinite expansion, and yet we are well aware that it is physically impossible to extrapolate the functioning of the industrialized world to the rest of the planet. Are we in some way like those compulsive collectors who accumulate objects until they are forced out of the house, now uninhabitable? Man forced out of the world by his creations.

Communism claimed to resolve the contradiction by conferring meaning on the work of all men. While accepting that it was caught in the flux of history, it had the Promethean ambition of raising itself above this flux, and putting an end to history by inventing a truth out of social relations. We are more modest; we, too, claim to "put an end to history," but by the disappearance of the battle of ideas, in a world that is sufficiently well organized for the ambition of "the truth" to have become unnecessary.

Nomads of modernity that we are, weary of the endless movement that progress has imposed on us for two centuries, we aspire to a little rest. The search for truth weighs on us, like an unwieldy piece of baggage that has become superfluous, not to say dangerous. Do we perhaps secretly hope that by renouncing it, we will escape the headlong rush we are caught up in? Must we accept that there is tranquillity only in slumber, and that human anxiety will be for a long time a subterranean river?

We have a revolution to accomplish, and this revolution is not of a political order, but a spiritual one. It is no good lamenting the crisis of the Enlightenment, and we must accept the fact that we are reaching the end of the institutional age of power. We will not be able to see it go without regrets. Its capacity to organize and simplify complex structures is exceptional: it will have succeeded, for nearly two centuries, in accompanying the unprecedented development of industrial society. The social ramifications of the age have multiplied infinitely, without throwing into question the fundamental principles of the institutionalization of power, and institutional organization has not yet slowed down the enrichment of social structures. Enterprises have grown, labor unions have developed, entire sectors of the economy have disappeared, and others have replaced them, and the very scale of these upheavals has seemed to demonstrate that only the institutionalization of power—in nation-state and parliamentary democracy—had sufficient flexibility to adapt to a society in perpetual change.

We see today that what we believed were definitive victories have been called into question by the development of the circuits of power. We have built on sand, and the foundations are crumbling. The great shibboleths of yesterday—democracy, liberty—ring hollow. Thrown into disarray, we have a choice between two attitudes. The first is to return to the origins of the institutional order that is disappearing, and to search, with broad agreement on some universal principles, for the foundations of a new religion, the natural law without which there is no law. This book has shown all the hazards of such a trajectory. We are no longer in the Age of the Enlightenment, and there is no longer a political order capable of establishing values. To make law, our religion thus risks being only a sleight of hand that will not long distract us. We will become the fastidious guardians of a well-oiled mechanism, but this sad ploy will not fill the central emptiness. A dangerous strategy because, in its apparently tolerant universality, it in fact leaves the door open for all sorts of illusions.

The other path, which we have tried to follow, is to contemplate reality head-on, to take stock of the end of the Age of Enlightenment and, only then, to try to save what can be saved. How far back should we go? Some have suggested to the Middle Ages and its Holy Roman Empire, but there is no Holy Empire without Christianity, and we should no doubt go much further still, to return to the stoics of antiquity who, after the decline of the city, were able to infuse liberty with a more philosophical than political meaning.

The most one can hope for from the unfolding imperial age is in fact that it resemble the Roman empire of Hadrian and Marcus Aurelius: like the empire, it should not claim either to elevate itself to the heavens or to appropriate the heavens for its earthly purposes. It would accept being only a functional mode, and knowing that that is all it is. That will be its fragility and its grandeur. There is thus no political recipe for confronting the dangers of the postpolitical age.

It is in this sense that the revolution to be accomplished is of a spiritual order. The debates of the future will focus on the relationship of man with the world: they will be ethical debates, and through them, perhaps, politics may one day be born again, in a process that will start from the bottom, from local democracy and the account that a community will give of itself, and proceed upward. The process will be the same whether in those areas of the world where democracy has never taken root (like the former Soviet Union) or in those where it is close to exhaustion. The solidarity that should permit us to overcome communal withdrawal will thus at the outset not be "political"; it will find its foundation in a feeling of common responsibility, in face of a world whose limits must circumscribe human ambition.

The ecological movement, in contrast with the defenders of the environment who came before it, declares that it refuses to make human beings the measure of all things, and seeks to decipher the rules of an order that is greater than we are. As long as it manages to free itself from the temptation of anthropocentrism and from that of replacing the ideology of the rights of man by that of the rights of blades of grass, it will perhaps provide new scope for revising the definition of the human community. In another way, medical progress, by liberating us from the hazards of genetics, forces us to reply to questions that we have never asked ourselves, and to redefine the respective fields of the individual and of society. We no longer know what liberty is, in the sphere too long inhabited by politics. Are we going to rediscover it, in a profound and new sense, in these unknown lands that are opening up to human ingenuity? At a time when geography still had a meaning, North America was the locus of the principal political experience of the institutional age. Perhaps those still unknown continents, ecology and bioethics, will finally permit the imperial world to engage in the debate over principles that it must have to acquire a meaning.

To make such a step possible, it will take some individuals, "wise men" capable of thinking through the finite world that has again become our common lot. This premise would be obvious to a sage of antiquity, but is strange and unrealistic naïveté in our institutionalized world, in which we expect everything of the social mechanism.

The end of the Age of the Enlightenment, and of its ambition to reveal the order of reason through politics, will not necessarily entail a renunciation of reason and a return to obscure passions. But to avoid this risk, we must find wisdom again today—in the stoic sense of the word—in order to preserve independence of the spirit not only from the police of dictators but from the impoverishment of consciences.

This will be no mean endeavor; this age is in fact generally tolerant, and it will consider picturesque rather than dangerous those who choose—like the Japanese hermits, their long hair whitened by solitude—not to "conform." How difficult it will be to plant one's feet on firm ground—in brief, to take seriously the freedom of the spirit, like those in Berlin and Moscow who risked their lives in a fight in which the search for truth was still a political act.

EPILOGUE

Three years have passed since the publication of the French edition of this book, and the broad outlines of the new world have begun to take shape. I retract nothing from my initial diagnosis, and if I have erred, it is out of timidity: I did not always dare to follow through the logic of my own conclusions, and I sometimes recoiled from the consequences of the hypotheses I was advancing.

Let us look at the world as it is, and as it is preparing to become. The resurgence of national ambitions has not strengthened the nation-states—far from it. With a few exceptions, sub-Saharan African states have become even more fragile. Rwanda, for example, has shown what can happen to a human community when it is deprived of a political framework. For the victims of Rwanda, whether hacked to death by machetes or felled by cholera, the distinction between natural calamities and those caused by human activities has been abolished. In the North, as well, the tendencies that I began to sketch out three years ago have been accentuated. Russia, the European Union, and the United States are all experiencing the same difficulty: that of redefining their identity.

The reemergence of a Russian nation is not a sign that the nation-states are gaining strength, even if the resurgence of an irredentist Russian ultranationalism permits a facile comparison with Weimar Germany. A closer examination of the situation in Russia reveals the limitations of such an analogy: on the periphery of the power struggles at the apex of the state, struggles in which analysis of the "private" interests of each actor often entails as many explanations as a classical political analysis, another Russia is in the process of emerging, one that increasingly eludes the influence of the central power. By provoking hyperinflation, its monetary indecision has deprived Russia for more than a year of its last effective leverage: budgetary power. Thousands of local actors obliged to "make do"—company functionaries, municipal or regional officials—have begun to construct a parallel society, not against the state, but alongside it. This development is reminiscent more of China after 1976—although the differences are great—than of pre-Hitler Germany. The hypothesis of a central power that could in the future, after a totalitarian coup d'état (or an election!), bring its imperial authority to bear on the periphery is fortunately not the most likely hypothesis, even if it cannot be discarded outright. The centers of autonomous power have been consolidated, and a totalitarian change of regime in Moscow would be more likely to lead to precarious alliances between great regional fiefdoms, punctuated by civil wars, than to a re-Stalinization or a "Hitlerization" of Russia.

Russia no longer follows Moscow's lead, and the questions this gives rise to stem from a new problematic: what will become of the disjunction between economic structures that acquire their own dynamic and political structures that do not manage to produce the monetary and regulatory foundations indispensable to the development of an economy? Must corruption be the only link between the worlds of economics and politics? Can the compromise that consists in buying the favor of state authorities with substantial bribes be a durable one? Does it not, in the long run, impose an excessive cost that will end by snuffing out the economic development of Russia, as the Mafia has stifled southern Italy? What principle can preserve the unity of a power that would now be no more than parasitical? Would being the bearer of a "Russian identity" suffice? Could a Russia parceled out between great fiefdoms, brought together more by the lust for gain than by a common political project, be strong enough not to break apart? One cannot expect a definitive reply to these questions for Russia any more than for China. But in both cases, the political struggles in which central power is at stake now appear as a secondary battle, almost an anecdotal one, of uncertain outcome. The real struggle is taking place elsewhere, apart from the political institutions, of which one can now only hope that they will not impede a movement engaged independently of them, and which is a threat to them.

In fact, Russia, in returning to its dimensions of the time of Peter the Great, has not become—as England or France did after they lost their colonies—the nation-state that it never was. In contrast to the old European kingdoms, which from the end of the Middle Ages abandoned the privilege of universality to the pope, holy Russia has never broken the thread that links it to Constantinople and the empire of the Orient. The communist empire was only one ephemeral incarnation of the imperial vocation that is inseparable from the Russian identity and its religious origins.

The old notion that a Russian feels safe within his own borders only as long as he can station his forces on all sides is thus more than a mean-spirited adage: it is the result of having disagreeable neighbors in an empire that has pretensions to universality. The idea of empire in this case recalls that of imperialism, under which not to extend one's frontiers is to risk watching them shrink. It is thus just as difficult to restrain one's own ambition as to forestall that of others, so long as one is no longer reasoning in the order of the particular.

Russia is thus confronted with the question of its limits, and the irony of history would have it that the European Union is confronted with the same question at the same time, if not on the same terms. This conjunction is not fortuitous, and there is a certain logic in the fact that the Christian states of the West are encountering the same difficulties as Russia, which is impregnated with the Christianity of the East, at the very moment at which they are trying to get beyond what separates them: the particularism of the nation-states, which were founded notably upon the exclusion from the political sphere of a universalist ambition that derives from the religious sphere. The construction of Europe, born of Christian democracy on the banks of the Rhine, in places where the memory of the Holy Roman Empire was still vivid, naturally soon rediscovers an imperial logic that brings it closer to Russia. At the point that the Western Europeans become dissatisfied with their national destinies, they rediscover a question that they would have liked to attribute simply to geography: it was more convenient and more reassuring to think that it was the immensity of the steppes and the uncertainty of the course of the great rivers of Siberia that prevented Russia from clearly establishing its borders, while the much-inscribed countryside of the old

Europe seems to lend itself more easily to a careful, precise de-marcation. However, there lies in this difficulty, now common both to Russia and to the European Union, far more than a simple by-product of geography: one does not easily circumscribe an ambition that has the pretension to be universal.

Still more seriously, it is not only that Russia and the European Union must pose the question of their boundaries, but they must ask the question as they meet—as the empire of the West encoun-tered the empire of the East in the past. Europe in the year 2000 thus runs into a problem it already confronted more than a mil-lennium ago. How would Russia accept exclusion from Europe, and on what grounds would Europe cut itself off from Russia? It is certainly easy to establish that the immense difficulties in which Russia finds itself do not realistically permit of the likelihood that it will join the European Union in the foreseeable future. But the question that is posed to Europeans is different and, indeed, en-tirely novel: should the yoking of Russia and the European Union in some larger association be a legitimate objective for the Euro-pean Union? As unlikely as that may seem, Europeans cannot ef-fectively escape the question, for the end of the cold war leaves them, whether they like this new responsibility or not, a margin of influence over Russia. It has thus become impossible for Europe to reconcile itself to accepting its eastern frontier. It is now up to Europe to define that frontier, and to ask, without hypocrisy, whether Russia has a part to play in the European design.

To put the question thus is to force oneself to state the dual im-possibility both of excluding Russia and of including it: in other words, the current impossibility of building a United States of Eu-rope on the model of the United States of America. Just as Germany could never become a federated state as long as Prussia was too powerful to become a member of the federation, so Europe as a political entity cannot wholeheartedly embrace a Russia that would dominate it. But the experience of relations between Prussia and the other German peoples, and in particular with Austria, also teaches us that there is nothing more unstable than two political projects that claim to embody the same identity. To claim to stabilize relations between an expanded European Union—excluding Russia—and Russia, by making partnership and cooperation an ultimate goal, is only a temporary response.

In one scenario, the European Union and Russia will consolidate themselves progressively, like two independent political entities. The resulting search for a security based on equilibrium will lead infallibly to mistrust followed by confrontation, as a result of the two protagonists being prevented by different strategic situations (i.e., Russia's need to defend the longest border in the world) from agreeing on the definition of equilibrium. In another scenario, a "cooperative partnership" between the European Union and Russia in fact implies the establishment of relationships of interdependence, on the model of what has been accomplished between the current members of the European Union. This could only amount to a phase that would leave intact the problem of the common finality of the European Union and Russia.

The United States, itself "deprived of enemies," is no more likely to avoid the question of redefining itself. Certainly, its identity, unlike that of the old nations of Europe, has not been forged in struggles with its neighbors, and U.S. involvement throughout the world, from Korea to Berlin, has been as much a response to moral considerations as to strategic imperatives. It remains the case that, for the first time in U.S. history, the logic of the nation's interests does not map onto its principles, and the United States, now attached to the rest of the world by myriad economic and human ties, cannot take refuge in an isolation that it has always dreamed of as an escape from the difficult choices in which the European nations have more practice. This is a novel situation that will lead to profound reevaluations and the subsequent transformation of the idea the United States has of itself. The energy of the American people has been fueled by a dual motivation: to offer a model of a new society that welcomes and gives a second chance to all the world's unfortunates; and to remake the world. But today, confronted like other developed countries with the pressure of migration created by the gulf between the rich and the poor, a gulf rendered more visible by the globalization of communication, the United States hesitates between an isolation that is contrary to its ideal and an openness that it can no longer master. The United States no longer offers a model to the world, but nonetheless still wants to change the world. Should it abandon that ambition as well?

Such a renunciation would be formidable not only for all those who, from European nations to Japan, have lazily consigned to their American ally the task of ensuring a little order, but also, more fundamentally, for the United States itself, now deprived of a truly federating project. It is not that the American national sentiment is threatened with extinction: on the contrary, seen from the old nations of Europe, which have too long a memory to ignore the dangers of nationalism, and too many "national" habits of mind to feel the need to reaffirm their national identity at every opportunity, the vigor of American "nationalism" tends to come as a surprise. But that is precisely the danger: an identity that affirms itself without the underpinning of a great collective project runs the risk of hardening into fanaticism—arrogant self-affirmation taking the place of a true ambition.

That is the crux of the difficulty of the period into which we have entered: the populations continue to want to recognize each other as nations, but the nations—even the most powerful of them all, the United States—no longer have the capacity, in a global world, of protecting the peoples whose destiny they claim to embody from the uncertainties of the outside world that have irreversibly irrupted into what used to be called their domestic affairs. Given competition from faraway countries, given the migration of poverty and terrorism, it has become as impossible to control the world that surrounds us as it is to ignore it. And the gulf between the nation as a locus of identity and the nation as a locus of power is formidable, for the natural temptation is to compensate with the complacent exaltation of one's identity what the nation has lost in effective power over the real.

How can we escape these dangers, and how can we prepare human communities for the new global world while preserving liberty and the values that, for a few centuries, have inspired the best of our past?

The French edition of this book bears a pessimistic title, *La fin de la démocratie,* which has led to some misunderstanding. With the brutal affirmation of this statement, I simply wished to indicate that human liberty could not be reduced to an institutional and juridical arrangement. Laws and institutions are an essential condition of liberty, but it is dangerous to believe that by themselves, they can ensure liberty, and that a human community is a sort of complicated clock whose cogs it is sufficient to oil. This illusion is at the root of the troubles of contemporary democracy, in which individuals are both free and incapable of exercising their freedom: the clock no longer has a mainspring.

The effort that must be undertaken is thus a double one: it is certainly a question of adapting institutions to the new globality, and of inventing new political forms, which cannot simply be a transposition to a continental or intercontinental level of the experience of the nation-states. For even the federated states, which by distributing power between different levels no doubt provide a part of the solution, obey a territorial principle ill-suited to our global world. But this political invention—which the European Union will have to attempt in the coming years if it wants to continue to progress; which Russia and China will have to experiment with if they are not to come unstuck; and which the United States will be wrong to ignore—is only half of the response.

It is also necessary to rediscover that a human community is not only a political notion but a philosophical and religious one. Having lost the comfort of our geographical boundaries, we must in effect rediscover what creates the bonds between humans that constitute a community. This rediscovery has hardly begun, and it will have to go further than the analysis of the dislocation of political societies—which is the subject of this book. In other words, we must concentrate on the careful observation both of the basic elements that contribute to the creation of a society and of the developments that affect them today: the relationships between men and women, between parents and children, the transformation of the very idea of the family, the redefinition of the notion of knowledge and education, the dislocation of the relationship between work and leisure, between middle age and old age. On all these levels, the century that is ending has brought more change than the millennium that preceded it. The optimistic nineteenth century, which even at the height of the triumph of the nation-state and of modern democracy had perhaps sensed its own precariousness, had hoped that science would furnish a response, and the stupid twentieth century thought it had found it. The result was the most terrible accumulation of barbarity since human beings have had the memory of their humanity. The scientific ambition of discovering the truth about society, and of deducing ideal political structures from it, has much to do with the destructive power of the two totalitarianisms that have shared this century: communism and Nazism.

We must try today to learn from our mistakes: not to stop casting the objective gaze of the savant on social phenomena to better understand the relationship between family structures, work, and technology, but to recognize at the same time the impossibility of having a global and totalizing vision of our collective destiny. For we cannot pretend to escape from the human collectivity, and to see it from the perspective of an inhabitant of Sirius. Our knowledge is like a sphere of expansion in the infinity of the unknown. By increasing in size, it does not, as the cliché has it, push back the frontiers of the unknown, for the infinite has no frontiers. It simply increases the extent of our contacts with the unknown: our awareness of our ignorance must increase in proportion to the extension of our knowledge. The progress that we can accomplish in the comprehension of human societies is thus vast, but it does not—far from it—eliminate the problematic character of all social constructions.

By positing the end of a certain political form, I shocked all those who imagined that there was a truth about society and a culmination of history, and that this culmination was democracy. In fact, I wanted first of all to posit the precariousness and contingency of all political forms, and if I stressed the features that differentiate the world that is beginning from the world that we have known, it was to explore, by contrast, the scope of the possible, and not to suggest the inevitable course of things. This observation is neither pessimistic nor optimistic—or rather, like all considered reflection on human destiny, it is both at the same time. It is pessimistic, for the precariousness of institutions that have for two centuries been our reference points—the state, the nation, democracy—is not a fact that one can treat lightly. The extreme difficulty with which human beings build compromises and consolidate institutions renders their disappearance all the more disturbing, at the very moment at which those compromises and institutions seem to have achieved a sort of equilibrium. But there is optimism here, too, for social invention is never completed, and the development of technology, by multiplying contacts and networks, by changing the rules of power, multiplies possibilities, thus increasing the human capacity for evil as well as good.

Infinitely more knowledgeable than Socrates, but keepers of a fragmented knowledge parceled out among innumerable specialists, we are now capable of building all sorts of "virtual communities" that will liberate us from the constraints of geography, and from the traditional political structures that have for so long framed our actions. But we are no more advanced than Socrates when it comes to exercising new powers and giving direction to our actions. More powerful than Socrates, we are neither freer, nor more just, than he.

INDEX

Afghanistan, 3

Barthes, Roland, 80
Berlin Wall, 27, 121
Bosnia, 36
Britain, 6, 115
bureaucracy, 103, 107

capital, movement of, 10
Carter, Jimmy, 29
checks and balances, 30
China, 47, 79, 80
cold war, x, 135
communalism, 37, 40, 41, 43, 45
Communism, collapse of, ix, 125
conformity, 43, 44, 79, 81, 89, 120, 124
conservatism, 83
corporate culture, 84, 87, 89, 103
corporations, 60, 62, 64, 107
corruption, 101-9

decision making, 102
democracy, 25, 141
designers, 86
deterrence, 113-15
drugs, 3, 4

ecology movement, 128
Enlightenment, ix, xi, 79, 91, 92, 126, 127, 129
Europe: cultural differences with U.S., 52; future of, 49, 50; and geography, 5
European Parliament, 51
European Union, 49-51, 139; foreign policy, 53; frontiers, 58, 134, 135, 136; legislation in, 15

federalism, 16, 50, 52
France: concepts of sovereignty in, 19, 55; defense, 115; and Europe, 53; Gaullism, 88; hierarchy in, 19; public service in, 106, 107

Germany, 1, 53, 55
gridlock, political, 31
Group of Seven, 113

Holy Roman Empire, 134
humanitarian groups, 95, 96
Hussein, Saddam, 124

Ibn Saud, 39
immigrants, 36, 44, 48

"Imperial age," 8, 15, 47, 70, 74, 77, 83;
    and barbarians, 120; claims of, 127;
    fragility of, 83; and networks, 86;
    and religion, 95, 100
imperialism, 7
International Monetary Fund, 2
Iran, 93, 111
Iraq, 37
Islam, 93, 94, 97, 99
Israel, 37, 39-41, 42

Japan: archaism, 18; business world, 73,
    91; corruption in, 101, 105, 106;
    defense, 14; diffusion of power in, 30,
    71, 72, 78; homogeneity of, 43;
    identity, 6, 98; interwar period, 112;
    lobbyists in, 22; rules, 34; snobbery,
    84

Kafka, Franz, 80
Kuwait, 122

law: crafting of, 28, 127; as distinct from
    religion, 5, 99, 100; as operating
    procedure, 68, 138
lawyers, 70
Lebanon: civil war in, 34, 36, 38, 40;
    communalism, 39, 41; and drugs, 3;
    sovereignty, 42
liberal democracy, 30, 31
liberty, xi, 1, 67; definition of, 68, 70, 81;
    in the modern age, 74, 75, 122, 126,
    138, 139
lobbyists, 20-21, 28

manufacturing, 85
media, 27, 29, 30, 118
money, 84, 108

nation-states, xiii, 4; demise of, 34;
    economic underpinning of, 9;

military organization of, 110, 115;
    power in, 126, 135; in transition, 5, 7,
    14, 89, 123, 141; and violence, 113
nationalism, 1, 38, 52
neocolonialism, 2
"networked world," 58-61, 64, 77, 87,
    97, 103, 111, 117, 119, 124, 141
nonconformity, 81, 82
nuclear age, 113-15

Palestinians, 40-42
politics, 12; common space for, 17, 78,
    123; control over, 78; demise of, 23,
    34, 91, 140; foundation of values, 55
poverty, 96
professionalization, 31, 63
pyramid of power, xii, 49, 62, 83, 102

Reagan, Ronald, 27, 29
religion, 91-98, 123
Roman empire, xii, xiii, 5; barbarians,
    123; and Christianity, 91; citizenship,
    48; as universal, 56, 57, 65
rules, 33, 58, 69
Russia, 65, 112, 132, 133-36
Rwanda, 131

scientific research, 15
sovereignty, xii, 19, 50, 54, 55, 57, 118
Soviet Union: breakup of, 1, 36; defense,
    13, 115; and democracy, 128;
    nationalism in, 1
Syria, 40

tariffs, 59
taxation, 10-12
telecommunications, 8
television, 28
Thomas, Clarence, 69
totalitarianism, 121, 140

United Nations, 1
United States: budgetary process, 32;
    bureaucracy, 20; business world, 26;
    defense, 13, 14, 135, 136; as federation,
    16; identity of, 131-32, 136, 137;
    litigious society, 24, 72; melting pot,
    43; nationalism, 135; national
    interest, 22; politics in, 26, 68, 107,
    139; rearmament of, 29; Supreme
    Court, 52, 69; universal suffrage, 27

voting patterns, 32

Weber, Max, 117
World Bank, 2

Yugoslavia, 36, 118

Jean-Marie Guéhenno is currently France's ambassador to the European Union. A graduate of the Ecole Normale Supérieure and the Ecole Nationale d'Administration, he has chosen to pursue a career with the French Government in the Treasury Department and in diplomacy. Guéhenno was head of the Policy Planning Staff in the Foreign Ministry from 1989 to 1993, during which time he also taught a course on geopolitics at the Institut d'Etudes Politiques. He has been a contributor to numerous newspapers and magazines, including *Le Monde*, the *International Herald Tribune*, *Politique Etrangère*, and *Politique Internationale*.

Victoria Elliott is a copy editor on the foreign news desk at the *San Francisco Chronicle*, and worked for the *International Herald Tribune* and at *Newsweek* in Paris from 1976 to 1987. She has done several translations for the French publisher Flammarion.